T0318259

Transparency, Public Relations, and the Mass Media

This book is about media transparency and good-faith attempts of honesty by both the sources and the gatekeepers of news and other information that the mass media present as being unbiased. Specifically, this book provides a theoretical framework for understanding media transparency and its antithesis—media opacity—by analyzing extensive empirical data that the authors have collected from more than 60 countries throughout the world. The practice of purposeful media opacity, which exists to greater or lesser extents worldwide, is a powerful hidden influencer of the ostensibly impartial media gatekeepers whose publicly perceived role is to present news and other information based on these gatekeepers' perception of this information's truthfulness. Empirical data that the authors have collected globally illustrate the extent of media opacity practices worldwide and note its pervasiveness in specific regions and countries. The authors examine, from multiple perspectives, the complex question of whether media opacity should be categorically condemned as being universally inappropriate and unethical or whether it should be accepted—or at least tolerated—in some situations and environments.

Katerina Tsetsura, Ph.D., is a Gaylord Family Professor of Strategic Communication/Public Relations in the Gaylord College of Journalism and Mass Communication at the University of Oklahoma, USA. She has published over 80 peer-reviewed studies and serves as a member of the editorial board of the *Communication Theory, International Journal of Strategic Communication, PR Journal*, and *PR Review* journals, among others.

Dean Kruckeberg, APR, Fellow PRSA, is a professor in the Department of Communication Studies at the University of North Carolina at Charlotte, USA. He is co-author of *Public Relations and Community: A Reconstructed Theory* and *This Is PR: The Realities of Public Relations*. Kruckeberg is author and co-author of many book chapters and articles dealing with global PR and international PR ethics.

Routledge Focus on Public Relations

1 Transparency, Public Relations, and the Mass Media
Combating the Hidden Influences in News Coverage Worldwide
Katerina Tsetsura and Dean Kruckeberg

Transparency, Public Relations, and the Mass Media

Combating the Hidden Influences in News Coverage Worldwide

Katerina Tsetsura and
Dean Kruckeberg

Routledge
Taylor & Francis Group

LONDON AND NEW YORK

First published 2017 by Routledge

2 Park Square, Milton Park, Abingdon, Oxfordshire OX14 4RN

52 Vanderbilt Avenue, New York, NY 10017

Routledge is an imprint of the Taylor & Francis Group, an informa business

First issued in paperback 2020

Library of Congress Cataloging in Publication Data
CIP data has been applied for

ISBN: 978-0-415-88424-2 (hbk)
ISBN: 978-0-367-60745-6 (pbk)

Typeset in Time News Roman PS
by diacriTech, Chennai

Contents

Figures and Tables

Acknowledgements

This book has had a long, arduous, and sometimes circuitous journey to its fruition, representing a stream of research that extends well over a decade. Its genesis began when Frank E. Ovaitt, then president and CEO of the Institute for Public Relations, approached Dean Kruckeberg about a global study of "cash for news coverage". Dr. Kruckeberg was enthused about the idea, but had asked to bring into the project a promising Russian doctoral student at Purdue University, Katerina Tsetsura. The original study resulted in a research report that received considerable news coverage and attention worldwide:

> Kruckeberg, D., & Tsetsura, K. (2003, July 21). A composite index by country of variables related to the likelihood of the existence of "cash for news coverage". Gainesville, FL: Institute for Public Relations.

Mr. Ovaitt was the liaison between the researchers and the commissioning organizations, was a co-researcher of the original project, and remains an advocate for additional research worldwide. Indeed, an extensive stream of research has continued to this day, especially by Dr. Tsetsura, who has studied the phenomenon worldwide.

The authors acknowledge the assistance of a large number of graduate research assistants throughout the years as well as those who had commissioned the original study, former graduate students Anna Klyueva, who co-authored Chapter 5, and Kelsie Aziz, who co-authored a section in Chapter 7 of this book, the Institute for Public Relations (USA) and the International Public Relations Association (UK), and the sponsor of the original study, Hurriyet, a member of Dogan Media Group (Turkey). The authors also thank the editorial and production staff of Taylor & Francis for its guidance and efforts in making this book a reality.

Katerina Tsetsura and Dean Kruckeberg

1 An Incomplete Truth

- Purpose: To introduce the agenda for this book's discussion about media transparency and opacity in presenting news and other information that the mass media present as truth. To establish the conceptual framework of the book by examining and contextualizing the concepts of transparency and opacity, as well as truth, incomplete truth, and a lie, by identifying opacity in the news media as problematic for many reasons, emphasizing its harm to both individuals and to society-at-large. To introduce and examine the moral/ethical arguments against news media opacity.
- Scope: To illustrate the complexity of the ethical questions related to news media opacity.
- Method: To provide the context for the authors' argument for an "ideal state" of transparency by and between the discrete professionalized communities of public relations practitioners and journalists.
- Results: The reader will understand the concepts and phenomena examined in this book as well as the authors' arguments for an "ideal state" of transparency.
- Recommendations: The reader should reflect on the issue of news media opacity and is encouraged to consider and accept the thesis of the book.
- Conclusions: That media opacity is harmful to individuals and to society-at-large and should be discouraged, indeed not tolerated, in the news media worldwide; it can be combated by publicly declared and universally adhered-to ethical standards that require transparency within the professionalized communities of public relations practitioners and journalists.

Transparency, Public Relations, and the Mass Media

This book is about news media transparency in the presentation of news and other information that the news media present as *truth*. Specifically, we provide a theoretical framework for understanding news media transparency and its antithesis—media opacity—by reporting and analyzing data from more than sixty countries throughout the world. While transparency in the news gathering/dissemination process is inferred by news media throughout much of the world, media opacity exists to greater or lesser extents worldwide. Lack of transparency allows powerful hidden interests to influence news media gatherers and disseminators, whose publicly perceived role is to present news and other information based on these gatekeepers' perception of this information's *truth*. Empirical data we have collected over the years illustrate the range and varying extents of media opacity worldwide as well as its pervasiveness in specific regions and countries. From multiple perspectives, we examine the complex question of whether media opacity should be categorically condemned as being universally inappropriate and unethical or whether it should be accepted—or at least tolerated—in some situations and environments.

What Is Transparency?

Before we examine other important concepts in this book, it is essential to define *transparency*. Wakefield and Walton (2010) noted:

> With the term transparency bantered around considerably today, it is easy to jump into the discussion; but the more difficult task is to dissect what transparency really means. Does transparency entail full disclosure of all information to all people at all times from every organization? Does transparency mean complete honesty and accuracy in information that should be disclosed? If so, what information should be disclosed and how or when that disclosure should take place? How are we to discern those conditions and boundaries? (p. 4)

This book examines news media transparency, particularly the news media's presentation of accurate, complete, and unbiased information in which no hidden influences exist in the *process* of gathering/disseminating news and other information that is presented as *truth*.

Thus, our definition of news media transparency is:

> No hidden influences exist in the *process* of gathering/disseminating news and other information that is presented as truth, or these influences have been clearly identified in the end-product in the media. To achieve media transparency, any influences that have been present should be clearly communicated in the end-product in the media. In other words, if a journalist gets influenced by a news source but then mentions this fact in the final product, such as an article or a broadcasting program, then the influence is transparent, or clear.

We define a conscious lack of transparency as *news media opacity*. Hidden influences might exist in the *process* of gathering/disseminating news and other information that is presented as truth, for example, any form of payment for news coverage or any influence on editorial and journalists' decisions that is not clearly stated in the finished journalistic product (Tsetsura & Grynko, 2009; Tsetsura & Kruckeberg, 2009). As an analogy, *transparency* exists in a lighted room, but *opacity* occurs when the lights are turned off and darkness results. What can be seen in the light is hidden in darkness. Perhaps the darkness hides nothing, but it certainly can hide a lot. Turning the lights off and thus bringing darkness into the room (purposeful opacity) creates a perfect condition for violating established rules and norms. Now, if someone punches you in the dark room, you may not know who has done it. Darkness hides the one who punched you so that the offending individual does not have to explain why he or she has done it. This punch, which has no consequences for the unknown offender, is only possible in the darkness. The same is true when we see media opacity through purposeful non-disclosure of influences on the news, which allows for non-transparent media practices, including but not limited to direct and indirect payments to the media from news sources, pressure from advertising departments, and financial pressure on the media.

What Is Truth?

Lack of transparency, that is, *opacity*, in the news gathering/dissemination process is a significant threat to people worldwide, both as citizens and as marketplace consumers. Consumers of news want—but do not always get or even expect—*truth* from their news media, and the presence of hidden influences suggest that truth is not being presented. Of course, *truth* is an abstract and complex concept. What is truth, and how can it be operationally defined? Is truth absolute? Is it even knowable or attainable to anyone other than to an omniscient being? And, do multiple and perhaps conflicting truths exist, which affirmative answer would seem logically inconsistent if truth were an absolute?

These larger questions can be left to philosophers. However, all of us as citizens and as marketplace consumers want and need the *truth* to make the best life decisions. We require accurate, complete, and unbiased news and other information that has been gathered and verified conscientiously and competently and that is presented fairly and in good faith by those who are attempting to achieve the ideal of objectivity with complete transparency in gathering/disseminating this information. In particular, those in democratic nation-states need accurate, complete, and unbiased news and information from impartial gatekeepers to inform public opinion for citizens' self-governance. Thus, for the purposes of this book, the definition of truth is:

> Accurate, complete, and unbiased information that has been gathered and verified conscientiously and competently and that is presented fairly and in good faith by those who are attempting to achieve the ideal of objectivity with complete transparency in gathering, analyzing, and presenting this information.

This definition acknowledges that a well-intentioned communicator who believes he or she is telling the "truth" may in fact be wrong, that is, the information later may be found to be incorrect or incomplete and thereby misleading. However, it is the *truth* as the communicator had believed it to be at the time and that the communicator had presented in good faith. Such a definition allows us to restrict our discussion to moral/ethical questions related to *truth* as it is presented in the *process* of gathering/disseminating news and other information.

If consumers of news are being presented incomplete truths by the news media, is such lying both blatant and pervasive? Or are citizens and marketplace consumers simply not being told the "whole truth" by some journalists and their news media because of hidden influences? This book provides evidence that news media *opacity*, that is, lack of transparency, is, in fact, pervasive in much of today's global news media and that this opacity oftentimes hides news media bribery and other influences that alter what we consume as news. Furthermore, news media opacity is exacerbated by today's changing business models of news media that are responding to people's use of new forms of communication technology. We argue for the exposure—and ideally the elimination—of these hidden influences in the news gathering/dissemination process, calling for transparency in particular by both public relations practitioners and journalists in their relationship to one another as they perform their discrete, but complementary, roles in society. Finally, this book will make specific recommendations to help ensure news media transparency that will reduce—or at least expose—news media bribery and other hidden influences that alter what we consume as "news".

The Most Insidious of Evils

The contention that consumers of news are not being told the truth because of news media bribery and other hidden influences that alter what we consume as "news" is a provocative—if not alarming—statement that begs clarification, substantiation, and contextualization. We have already defined *truth* as it is conceptualized in this book, noting that all of us as citizens and as marketplace consumers want and need *truth* to make the best life decisions.

But do the news media and their sources really lie? To answer this, we must define and examine the concept of a *lie*, which is arguably among the most insidious of evils because it is a violation of trust. Lying may be among the most reprehensible of acts because the liar is attempting to mislead the individual being lied to by attempting to create, but then exploit, trust. All of us are lied to myriad times throughout our lives, oftentimes inconsequentially, but sometimes resulting in dire consequences. At the interpersonal level, a lie may have encouraged us to have made a decision that we otherwise would have considered foolhardy had we known the "truth"; a victim's discovery of a lie may have resulted in emotional hurt, together with devastating feelings of betrayal, and such discovery may have prompted a painful realignment of that individual's personal beliefs as well as a recontextualization and reassessment of his or her memories. Deceitful lovers, unscrupulous salespeople, duplicitous colleagues, misleading advertisers, dishonest government officials—such liars can cause incalculable harm to the victims of their lies; furthermore, with lost innocence, a liar's victims may develop an unhealthy suspicion of all information providers, including those who may be worthy of these victims' trust.

Communication ethicists provide a range of perspectives and insights about lies and lying. These include Immanuel Kant's duty-bound (deontological) Categorical Imperative that advocates universal and absolute principles of truth and Sissela Bok's observation that lies add to the power of the liar while diminishing that of the deceived because the latter's choices are altered (Johannesen, Valde, & Whedbee, 2008). The concept of a lie remains morally complex; for example, some argue that the morality of—and tolerance for—lying may be culture-bound, suggesting that its ethicality must be contextualized within a specific culture (Johannesen et al., 2008; Sriramesh, 2009). Also, the act of lying in some situations is oftentimes defended, for example, morally compelling reasons may exist to tell a lie. Scenarios might range from lying to save the life of a potential victim of a death squad to the insincere utterance of a "white lie" to spare hurt feelings over inconsequential issues. However, despite situational moral justifications, these falsehoods remain lies by definition. Just as with truth, the definition of a lie must be viewed as an absolute, the presentation of information that the communicator believes to be untrue with the intent to deceive and/or mislead. Importantly, it is not the false information, itself, but the conscious intent of the communicator of a lie to deceive and/or mislead that is central to the definition of a lie as well as to any moral condemnation of the communicator of this lie. Thus, in this book, the conceptual definition of a *lie* is:

Information that the communicator knows to be false that is presented with the intent to deceive and/or mislead.

Despite the concept's moral complexity as well as its possible situational justifications, it is safe to say that most people do not enjoy being lied to because a lie disorients them at best and indeed can do them much harm. People make decisions based on information that is communicated to them, and a lie may result in decisions that otherwise may not have been made. When false information is communicated purposely, that is, with knowledge and with the intent to deceive and/or mislead, the *consumer* of that lie must be considered a victim because his or her decision-making is being influenced by deceitful and/or misleading communication of false information. The motive for communicating a lie usually is a self-perceived benefit for the liar or that individual's perception of a "greater good".

We do not contend that most news media blatantly and pervasively lie; however, global research presented later in this book suggests that the news and other information that the news media present as truth oftentimes do not satisfy this book's definition of *truth*. However, if truth is an absolute, and most news media do not blatantly and pervasively lie, can there be an imperfect truth, that is, information that is not the *truth*, but neither is it a *lie*, the latter which we say is also an absolute? Yes, but it is better to call it an *incomplete truth*, suggesting that the news and other information that the news media present as truth may be by-and-large accurate, but that the news media have intentionally omitted contextualizing information, for example, that a source paid for placement of the information or that other hidden influences may have altered the presentation or content of this information with the intent to deceive and/or mislead. While semantically a *lie* and an *incomplete truth* may appear by-and-large synonymous, we prefer the concept of an *incomplete truth* to examine news media bribery and other hidden influences that alter what we consume as "news" and other information that is presented as *truth*. Both lies and incomplete truths can exist because of media opacity, the condition of darkness in the room. However, focusing on the concept of an *incomplete truth* allows us to examine the ethical validity of intentionally communicating, if not a blatant lie, certainly less than the "whole truth". It is with good reason that witnesses in courts of law must swear to "tell the truth, the whole truth, and nothing but the truth".

In this book, the definition of an *incomplete truth* is:

> News and other information that is being presented as truth may be by-and-large accurate, but the news gatherer/disseminator has intentionally omitted contextualizing information or has purposely failed to identify influences that have altered the presentation of this information with the outcome of deceiving and/or misleading.

Recognize that this outcome may not always be by intent. Furthermore some journalists may argue that consumers of the news and other information know these influences exit, so journalists and their news media do not need to disclose that they were influenced by a government or perhaps by those owning or managing these news media.

Of course, many communicators do not achieve—and oftentimes purposely resist—the communicative ideal of truth, and consumers of their communication don't (or at least shouldn't) expect truth from these individuals as this book defines the concept. The astute consumer of information is rightfully cautious, if not overtly distrustful, of the high-pressure salesperson who wants to sell an automobile and the politician who is pandering for a vote—these communicators may provide by-and-large truthful information to support their arsenal of persuasive messages, that is, they may not pervasively communicate blatant lies, but they are purposive communicators to whom high levels of trust in the *truth* of their communication may not be deserved. Interestingly, some might argue that such communicators may be ethical within their situational roles. Johannesen et al. (2008) argued:

> Beyond a general implied ethical contract, various types of communication settings, communicator roles, and each specific situation may have unspoken expectations that help define the ethical relationship between communicator and audience. (p. 13)

Some might argue that such communication may be ethical, even if it is *incomplete truth*, because the consumer of the information understands the situational roles of the car salesperson and politician and should be able to correctly interpret the communication setting and the communicator's role as not worthy of trust.

It's about Trust

Can communicators of intentionally persuasive messages, that is, in which the motive for communication extends beyond the presentation of accurate, complete, and unbiased information, communicate *truth* as it is defined in this book? Some might argue that they may if they are transparent in their motives, that is, if their roles are obvious. We know the car salesperson who needs to meet his or her monthly quota may purposely provide incomplete information; he or she will not be unbiased and perhaps will not be entirely accurate about the merits of the automobile he or she wants to sell you, and he or she likely will not be completely forthcoming about alternative choices at the dealership across the street. Perhaps at some expense, we have learned to identify and interpret these communicators' situational roles and will attempt to defend ourselves accordingly against *spin*, recognizing the intent of the communicator who wishes us to believe or to do something. Ultimately, *trust* becomes a critical concept in our determination of *truth*, in our recognition of a *lie*, and in our caution about an *incomplete truth*. *Trust* in this book is:

> The belief in the truth of a communicator's message.

Whom do people trust? Of course, those whom they perceive to be telling the truth. Valentini and Kruckeberg (2011) argued:

> ... (T)rust can only exist where it is deserved, i.e such trust cannot be betrayed. A requisite of trust is the reasonable prediction and anticipation of an action by an actor based on that actor's prior behavior and other communication. (p. 99)

Although we may be often lied to or told incomplete truths, we nevertheless expect most of our daily communication, and perhaps the vast majority of inconsequential communication, to be *truthful*. Johannesen et al. (2008) noted the assumption that people would be overall truthful in their communication. Certainly, communicators who are intentionally persuasive may not be telling the truth as we have defined it. They may be blatantly lying on occasion, but, more commonly, their communication may be an incomplete truth because that communicator has intentionally omitted contextualizing information or because hidden influences have altered the presentation of this information with the outcome, and oftentimes the intent, to deceive and mislead the consumer of this information. And in our daily lives, much of the *incomplete truth* that is communicated to us may not be gravely consequential, and most is easily recognizable.

However, in our role as citizens, the truth and our decisions about whom to trust become critically important and may not be easily discernable. Also, as marketplace consumers, our economic welfare and sometimes our physical safety may be at stake in our determination of what is truth, what is an incomplete truth, and what is a blatant lie. Our decisions about whom and what to trust become of utmost importance.

Whom Should We Be Able to Trust?

Whom *should* we be able to trust to provide us with truth so that we can make informed life decisions in our roles as citizens and as marketplace consumers? In modern societies, the ready answer is the news media, that is, organizations that disseminate "news" to a general audience, today through channels of communication that include newspapers, radio and television stations, the Internet and its websites, and the various forms of social media.

For multiple reasons, the news media are universally important as a societal institution; however, the role of the news media becomes essential in free and democratic societies because news media as an institution have a critical role in safeguarding us both as citizens and as marketplace consumers. These news media should attempt to earn our trust because their societal role is to present the truth. However, considerable evidence worldwide suggests that news media often provide *incomplete truth* because of hidden influences that can exist because of media opacity that prevents the disclosure of these influences, for example, cash for news coverage in Russia, advertising in the news media in exchange for news coverage in the USA, and gifts, free meals, and free trips to journalists and editors in exchange for publication in China, Nigeria, Peru, Ukraine, and the USA (Ristow, 2010).

We Continue to Rely on the News Media

Tsetsura and Kruckeberg (2009) noted that, in today's global society, the compression of time and space has resulted in increased social-political-economic-cultural complexity worldwide; furthermore, contemporary communication technology is making seemingly infinite amounts of information from multiple sources readily available that help create our individual worldviews from which we form our beliefs, attitudes, and opinions that directly influence the decisions that we make. Vujnovic and Kruckeberg (2010) observed that rapidly developing communication technologies:

> ... (a) allow and encourage the increasing compression of time and space, (b) make global communication unprohibitively inexpensive, (c) overwhelm people with information, and (d) intermingle traditional vetted sources of information with user-generated content (UGC) that may be suspect in source credibility and nontransparent regarding agenda. (p. 217)

Indeed, some have questioned the continuing relevance of the traditional news media, pondering how news media can even be defined today—certainly a valid question in an era in which social media have allowed infinite numbers of messages to be sent from myriad sources using inexpensive channels of communication without any constraints of time and space.

Kruckeberg and Tsetsura (2004) reflected on the changing role of journalism when they questioned whether each person would become his or her own journalist; whether the concept of journalism would become deprofessionalized, with longstanding professional practices and ethical values becoming passé; whether the concepts of news and news values would any longer have meaning; and whether the agenda-setting role of the traditional mass media would become increasingly eroded because of the immense amount of readily available information.

In the 1830s during the advent of the "Penny Press" in the United States, news from a political party press that had been openly and admittedly ideological evolved into a commodity sold by a commercial press that was dependent upon advertising. Capitalist newspaper publishers who relied on advertising revenues did not attempt to align themselves with the ideologies of their readers, the consumers of this news, at least to the extent that it would impact their profits. News became a commodity that had value and could be sold at a profit, and of course the range and number of consumers could be increased by giving news a value as a commodity regardless of readers' political or ideological beliefs. Fairness and objectivity were profitable for a publisher who could promote political beliefs in the editorial and op-ed sections, while assuring that the monetary value of news was not diminished by biases caused by lack of fairness and objectivity. Of course, editorial decisions were influenced by multiple forces, some undoubtedly hidden, but the overall decision-making of news gatherers and disseminators was primarily guided by the value of this commodity of news to as many consumers as possible. Today's news "values" became the norm: a story's significance, that is, how a reported incident affected the reader, and the readers' potential interest in a story, for example, the prominence of its protagonists and antagonists, and its timeliness, proximity, unusualness, and human interest (Craig, 2003, 2006). Although such news "values" became institutionalized and normative, the influences in an ideological press that were once transparent might now be hidden in the news gathering/disseminating process.

Today, we continue to rely upon—if not always trust—the news that is presented in the newspapers that we read, the television news programs that we watch, the news programs of radio stations to which we listen, and the news media Internet sources that we monitor, due in some part because we have few alternatives. It is because of this role that journalism as a professionalized occupation and the news media as a societal institution have value and indeed are essential. As Kruckeberg and Tsetsura (2004) have predicted:

> It seems almost certain that an overwhelming majority of people will continue to rely on journalists as experts and on news media … to

gather and to report the news. This majority will depend on the gate-keepers of an established press to set news agenda, to grade news, and to provide informed comment about current events. (p. 89)

Journalists' Universal Role Remains to Provide Truth

We argue that journalists' universal role remains to provide *truth* as this book has defined it; journalists' ability to gather and to disseminate this truth through the news media is what gives their professional occupation and the news media critical importance and essential roles in modern society. These roles remain despite—and become all the more important because of—the myriad sources of information that are available today. Indeed, today's proliferation of readily available information from non-journalists and non-news media sources through the Internet has caused Kruckeberg and Tsetsura (2004) to question:

> As in centuries past, when emerging Protestant religions declared that everyone could become his own priest and now could read his own Gutenberg Bible, is today's communication "revolution" more accurately a "reformation" in which each person can be his or her own journalist within a global milieu of interactive multimedia? (p. 85)

Their answer was no; the reality is that most of the seemingly infinite content of the Internet in the new media is *incomplete truth*. Much of this content is once again overwhelmingly ideological; while this information might appear credible, it does not satisfy the criteria of accurate, complete, and unbiased information, and consumers of this content increasingly recognize this. Indeed, a healthy mistrust has resulted among consumers of the overwhelming amount of content that is communicated on these channels of communication. Those searching for truth on the World Wide Web can readily find questionable sources of information, quickly appreciating that vigilance and suspicion are required and concluding that they, and not professional journalists, must be responsible for determining truth from among these myriad sources. Undoubtedly, the Internet, the World Wide Web, and the new social media—with their conflicting, sometimes incredible, and oftentimes suspect information—have performed a tremendous service to society by taking trust away from the channels of communication and redirecting consumers' attention to the content providers of these channels—ultimately reinforcing the need for professional journalists and their news media. Social media have reintroduced and reinforced a healthy skepticism about the integrity of the media, which—it must be re-emphasized—remain only a channel of communication. Ironically, the Internet may have done society a great service in creating a healthy skepticism about the truthfulness of media and in reassigning responsibility to the users of these media.

Despite immense changes brought about by the Internet, the World Wide Web, and social media, the normative *role* of news media remains the same, and thus *news values* must remain the same and the *journalist's role*, which Kruckeberg and Tsetsura (2004) likened that to a mediating priest, must remain the same. Some important work has been done in journalism in the area of understanding the role, function, and place of journalists in modern society (Singer, 2006a). Many scholars have addressed the process of conceptualizing values and norms by modern journalists as they engage in information gathering and in ethical decision making as they work on stories (Craig, 2006, 2008, 2011). The concepts of truth and transparency are central to journalism, although recently these are often challenged by the growing presence of professional and non-professional communicators online (Singer, 2006a, b, 2007). Also remaining the same must be the guardianship of media transparency and concerns about media opacity that allows hidden influences to create *incomplete truth* in what we consume as "news", that is, in which complicity between journalists and sources such as public relations practitioners, as well as advertisers, corrupt news media's presentation of truth.

Of course, we recognize that journalists and their news media worldwide are influenced by multiple forces that impede their ability to tell the truth, and oftentimes these forces are beyond news media's ability to control: oppressive governments, restrictive laws, and a full range of threats and hostile actions that prevent journalists from reporting *truth* in their presentation of news and other information. These forces of oppression are not what this book is about; rather, this book examines the phenomenon of media opacity that oftentimes hides complicity between news gatherers/disseminators and their sources, for example, public relations practitioners and advertisers, which has allowed news media bribery and other hidden influences to alter what we consume as "news".

Summary

This book began with a provocative—if not alarming—contention that consumers of news are not being told the truth because of news media opacity that has allowed bribery and other hidden influences to alter what we consume as "news". To prepare to examine this phenomenon that is a significant threat to people worldwide, both as citizens and as consumers, several concepts have been defined:

News media transparency:	No hidden influences exist in the *process* of gathering/disseminating news and other information that is presented as *truth*.
News media opacity:	Hidden influences exist in the *process* of gathering/disseminating news and other information that is presented as truth, for example, any form of payment for news coverage or any influence on editorial and journalists' decisions that is not clearly stated in the finished journalistic product.
Truth:	Accurate, complete, and unbiased information that has been gathered and verified conscientiously and competently and that is presented fairly and in good faith by those who are attempting to achieve the ideal of objectivity with complete transparency in gathering, analyzing, and presenting this information.
Lie:	Information that the communicator knows to be false that is presented with the intent to deceive or mislead.
Incomplete truth:	News and other information that is being presented as truth may be by-and-large accurate, but the news gatherer/disseminator has intentionally omitted contextualizing information or has purposely failed to identify influences that have altered the presentation of this information with the outcome of deceiving and/or misleading.
Trust:	The belief in the truth of a communicator's message.

For multiple reasons, news media are universally important as a societal institution, safeguarding us both as citizens and as marketplace consumers. Despite immense changes brought about by the Internet, the World Wide Web, and social media, we have argued that the normative *role* of news media remain the same and that *news values* as well as the *journalist's role* must remain the same. If anything, journalists and their news media will have greater importance because we as citizens and marketplace consumers, drowning in a sea of information, will rely increasingly on professional journalists and news media that can be trusted to set news agenda, to grade news, and to provide informed comment. To earn this trust, journalists and news media must have transparency, rather than news media opacity that allows hidden influences to create *incomplete truth* in what we consume as "news". Although multiple forces impede journalists and their news media's ability to tell the truth, this book examines media opacity that hides complicity between news gatherers and disseminators and their sources, which has allowed news media bribery and other hidden influences to alter what we consume as "news". The next chapter will further investigate the phenomenon of media opacity.

References

Craig, D. (2011). *Excellence in online journalism: Exploring current practice in an evolving environment.* Thousand Oaks, CA: Sage.

Craig, D. A. (2008). Journalists, government, and the place of journalism across cultures. *Journal of Mass Media Ethics, 23,* 158–161.

Craig, D. (2006). *The ethics of the story: Using narrative techniques responsibly in journalism.* Lanham, MD: Rowman & Littlefield.

Craig, D. (2003). The promise and peril of anecdotes in news coverage: An ethical analysis. *Journalism & Mass Communication Quarterly, 80,* 802–817.

Johannesen, R. L., Valde, K. S., & Whedbee, K. E. (2008). *Ethics in human communication.* Long Grove, IL: Waveland Press, Inc.

Kruckeberg, D., & Tsetsura, K. (2004). International journalism ethics. In J. C. Merrill & A. De Beer (Eds.), *Global journalism: Topical issues and media systems* (pp. 84–92). New York: Longman.

Ristow, B. (2010). *Cash for coverage: Bribery of journalists around the world.* A Report to the Center for International Media Assistance. Electronic version. Retrieved from http://cima.ned.org/sites/default/files/CIMA-Bribery_of_Journalists-Report.pdf.

Singer, J. (2007). Contested autonomy: Professional and popular claims on journalistic norms. *Journalism Studies, 8*(1), 79–95.

Singer, J. (2006a). The socially responsible existentialist: A normative emphasis for journalists in a new media environment. *Journalism Studies, 7*(1), 2–18.

Singer, J. (2006b). Partnerships and public service: Normative issues for journalists in converged newsrooms. *Journal of Mass Media Ethics, 21,* 30–53.

Sriramesh, K. (2009). The relationship between culture and public relations. In K. Sriramesh & D. Verčič (Eds.), *The global public relations handbook: Theory, research, and practice (Revised and expanded edition)* (pp. 52–67). New York: Routledge.

Tsetsura, K., & Grynko, A. (2009). An exploratory study of media transparency in Ukraine. *Public Relations Journal, 3*(2). Retrieved from www.prsa.org/prjournal/index.html?WT.ac=PRJournalTopNav.

Tsetsura, K., & Kruckeberg, D. (2009). Truth, public relations and the mass media: A normative model to examine media opacity. *Proceedings of the 12th International Interdisciplinary Public Relations Research Conference*, Miami, FL: University of Miami.

Valentini, C., & Kruckeberg, D. (2011). Public relations and trust in contemporary global society: A Luhmannian perspective of the role of public relations in enhancing trust among social systems. *Central European Journal of Communication*, *4*(1), 89–105.

Vujnovic, M., & Kruckeberg, D. (2010). Managing global public relations in the new media environment. In M. Deuze (Ed.), *Managing media work* (pp. 217–223). London: Sage.

Wakefield, R. I., & Walton, S. B. (2010). The translucency corollary: Why full transparency is not always the most ethical approach. *Public Relations Journal*, *4*(4), Retrieved from www.prsa.org/Intelligence/PRJournal/Archives/index.html#. VzYj-k3ru70.

2 Multiple Truths

- Purpose: To examine how journalists and news consumers' worldviews are comprised of an infinite number of variables that have uniquely molded each of us to be the individuals that we are and how these worldviews provide the foundations from which we form our unique perceptions of truth.
- Scope: To emphasize the importance of promoting ethical practices for educational and professional communities and of combating media opacity worldwide.
- Method: To define and examine additional concepts needed in this discussion and to raise questions and provide answers regarding individuals' pursuit of truth.
- Results: The reader will understand the importance of truth from journalists and their news media, which is only obtainable when media transparency exists.
- Recommendations: The reader will reflect on the issues involved in news media transparency and opacity as well as on truth, incomplete truth, and lies in the news media.
- Conclusions: The reader will understand the need for news media transparency.

Chapter 1 contended that consumers of news are often being told incomplete truth because *news media opacity* has allowed bribery and other hidden influences to alter what we consume as "news". As an analogy, *transparency* exists in a lighted room, but opacity occurs when the lights have been turned off and darkness results. What can be seen in the light is hidden in darkness. Perhaps the darkness hides nothing, but it certainly can hide a lot.

Several concepts were defined in the first chapter: *news media transparency*, *news media opacity*, *truth*, *lie*, *incomplete truth*, and *trust*. Despite the overwhelming amounts of information that are readily available to nearly everyone in today's information age, the news media remain essential as a societal institution to safeguard us as citizens and as marketplace consumers; in free and democratic societies in particular, journalists and their news media have a unique role that allows those societies' citizens to self-govern responsibly, and consumers in a marketplace economy need information from sources that they can trust to make wise life decisions. Seemingly counter-intuitively, we as citizens and as marketplace consumers will rely, not less so, but increasingly on professional journalists in their role and their news media as a societal institution because we have become overwhelmed, indeed oversaturated, with readily accessible information from sources ranging from WikiLeaks and corporate websites to myriad—oftentimes suspect or unknown—sources of conflicting and questionable, if not incredible, information. The ready availability of seemingly infinite amounts of information from sources on the World Wide Web as well as in the social media will not change the need for accurate, complete, and unbiased news and other information that has been gathered and verified conscientiously and competently and that is presented fairly and in good faith by those who are attempting to achieve the ideal of objectivity with complete transparency in gathering, analyzing, and presenting this information. Citizens and marketplace consumers will continue to need professional journalists and their news media to help set the news agenda, to grade the news, and to provide informed and impartial interpretation of current events as well as to help us make informed life decisions. Journalists' ability to gather and to disseminate *truth* gives their professional occupation not only an essential role, but also a unique responsibility in society; however, fulfillment of this role is contingent on the *trust* that journalists and their news media earn. And to earn this trust, journalists and their news media must be *transparent* because *news media opacity* allows and encourages hidden influences to alter what we consume as "news" and other information that we need to be able to trust.

Once again, what is truth, and can multiple truths exist? In the previous chapter, we qualified truth by noting that it is the truth the communicator believed to exist presented in good faith with no hidden influences that have altered its presentation. Yet any consumer of news who has examined multiple reports of the same news event or situation knows that different information is included and omitted in individual news stories. Also, the emphases, if not the perspectives, of journalists vary considerably, even though all may have attempted to conscientiously and competently gather and verify and then disseminate accurate, complete, and unbiased information. Journalism professors who assign a class to cover the same news event note this inevitable variance, as do law enforcement officers who interview witnesses to a crime. Indeed, anyone who asks a simple question, "What happened at yesterday's meeting?", will be given varying accounts, perspectives, and emphases by those who were in attendance.

In this sense, multiple truths exist because conscientious and competent journalists sample a range of sources, which oftentimes differ, and interpret this information from each journalist's unique perspectives. Individual journalists investigating the same news event or situation will have not only a different news-gathering experience, but will uniquely contextualize and interpret that news event or situation according to his or her unique worldview. Nevertheless, it is likely that each journalist is reporting the *truth* as he or she believes it to be, and in this sense there are multiple truths. One might suggest that such variance is not only inevitable, but arguably is good. Although these multiple truths certainly suggest that consumers of news should seek several reports of the same news event or situation to determine his or her own truth from all the information and interpretation that is available, these multiple truths should not be considered ethically problematic, even though they might indicate varying levels of competence and expertise among journalists.

To further confound this search for truth, we as consumers of news and other information sample these multiple truths to arrive at our own truth, contextualizing and ascribing meaning to news and other information according to the infinite number of values that have shaped our own unique "worldviews". As is the case with an individual news gatherer/disseminator, each news consumers' worldview is likewise comprised of an infinite number of variables that have uniquely molded that individual, which influences his or her perception of what is truth as he or she contextualizes and interprets multiple and sometimes conflicting truths in the news media. Thus, one might conclude that absolute truth may not exist and plausibly multiple truths have equal ethical validity.

Such arguments are irrelevant, however, in the consideration of *incomplete truth*. The *incomplete truth* that this book examines occurs when a news gatherer/disseminator has intentionally omitted contextualizing information or has purposely failed to identify influences that have altered the presentation of this information with the outcome of deceiving and/or misleading. *Incomplete truth* exists when *news media opacity* veils complicity between news gatherers/disseminators and their sources, cloaking news media bribery and other hidden influences that alter what we consume as "news". However, to further explore this phenomenon, we must better define some of the concepts that we have already been using as well as define other important concepts that we have yet to identify.

A major hidden influence that is cloaked by news media opacity is *pay-for-publicity*. Specifically, this is payment to news media and individual journalists for media coverage. Demand for *cash for editorial* by consumer news media to information subsidies providers is a more accurate, albeit much more cumbersome, descriptor of this practice that can be found globally (Kruckeberg & Tsetsura, 2003). The term *information subsidies* was originally conceived by communication scholar O. H. Gandy Jr. to label editorial content that public relations practitioners provide free of charge to media (Hunt & Grunig, 1994). *Editorial content* is synonymous with Newsom, Turk, and Kruckeberg's (2010, p. 384) definition of *editorial matter*, i.e., "The entertainment or educational part of a broadcast program or publication, exclusive of commercial messages". Examples include the news, feature, and editorial opinion sections of consumer news media, not including advertisements and commercials. *Consumer news media* are channels of communication that are devoted primarily to *news* dissemination to a general audience, and these channels of communication today not only include traditional newspapers, radio, and television stations, but also the Internet and its World Wide Web as well as the various social media, which in this book we refer to simply as *news media*.

Mencher (2011) noted that definitions of news may change, but identified two constant guidelines in defining news: "News is information about a break from the normal flow of events, an interruption in the expected, a deviation from the norm" and "news is information people can use to help them make sound decisions about their lives". *Newsworthiness* is "(t)he often unstated criteria that journalists use to determine which events and issues should become news reports, including timeliness, proximity, conflict, prominence, human interest, consequence, usefulness, novelty, and deviance" (Campbell, Martin, & Fabos, 2008, p. G-9). Newsom, Turk, and Kruckeberg (2010, p. 377) defined *advertising* as "Paid-for time or space, except in the case of public service announcements (PSAs) where the time and space are donated to a nonprofit organization". Campbell, Martin, and Fabos (2008, p. G-0) defined a *newshole* as "the space left over in a newspaper for news content after all the ads are placed". News—when it is accurate, complete, and unbiased information, has been gathered and verified conscientiously and competently, and is presented fairly and in good faith in an attempt to achieve objectivity—becomes a salable *commodity* that has value, which Guralnik (1980, p. 286) defined as "anything bought and sold; any article of commerce".

Gatekeepers are "editors, producers, and other media managers who function as message filters, making decisions about what types of messages actually get produced for particular audiences" (Campbell, Martin, & Fabos, 2008, p. G-6). Shoemaker, Eichholz, Kim, and Wrigley (2001, p. 235) note that *gates* are decision points at which items may be stopped or moved from section to section or from channel to channel, while *gatekeepers* are the individuals or sets of routine procedures that determine whether items pass through the gates.

Also needing definition is the concept of *journalism*, itself, especially in a twenty-first-century technological, multicultural, and global milieu. Kruckeberg (1995, pp. 78–79) discussed the complexities of journalism and the role of the journalist when he observed that we can be no more precise than to argue that "'journalism' is what 'journalists' do". He noted that a journalist could be a public affairs reporter of government activity or an advice columnist, an ideological interpreter of news for a propagandistic medium owned or sanctioned by an authoritarian government, or a reporter for a commercially "controlled" medium. *Journalism* is defined in this study as "the process of reporting news", and a *journalist* is someone who is engaged in this process for his or her primary livelihood.

However, given the difficulty of defining what journalism is in contemporary global society, consumer news media and their journalists/gatekeepers to a great extent must be defined according to *press systems*—which still vary tremendously throughout the world in this post-Cold War twenty-first century. Such systems may range from authoritarian to social responsibility to libertarian models (Kruckeberg, 1995, pp. 79–80). Siebert, Peterson, and Schramm (1956) identified four models of that time: authoritarian, libertarian, Soviet communist, and social responsibility theories, while Lowenstein (Merrill & Lowenstein, 1971; Mundt, 1991) modified this typology, identifying ownership types (private, multiparty, and government ownership) as well as five press philosophies. Other scholars have identified additional typologies.

However, Kruckeberg (1995) attempted to identify which media and messages should be included in a nation's press system when he excluded special interest periodicals and media controlled by public relations practitioners, marketing communicators, and the like:

> Helpful is the identification of a predominant *general* news orientation of qualifying media as a uniform and consistent threshold criterion. Public affairs reportage about journalists' respective governments likewise is a strong definitional component of such journalism as it is practiced in the general news media. (p. 79)

A *bribe* is anything, especially money, that is given or promised to induce a person to do something illegal or wrong or anything given or promised to induce a person to do something against his wishes (Guralnik, 1980, p. 176).

While it is important to understand these concepts as a foundation to understand *news media transparency* and *opacity* as well as *truth, incomplete truth*, and a *lie*, to simplify this book's discussion throughout the remainder of the book, many of the concepts defined above will not be used, and simpler—less onerous—labels will describe these concepts, in particular:

Media bribery: "Pay-for-publicity"; the payment to journalists and/or news media for media coverage that is presented as news that is ostensibly the *truth*, as defined in this book.

Media release: Information subsidy, that is, editorial content that public relations practitioners provide free of charge to media.

As noted, *news* is a *commodity* that has value to the consumers of news media when it is the *truth*. Of course, many barriers can impede journalists' ability to gather and news media's ability to disseminate truth; for example, journalists and their news media are influenced by multiple hostile forces of which journalists and their news media are hardly complicit. These may range from oppressive governments, to restrictive laws and the threat of physical harm from criminal cartels. Journalists and their news media are oftentimes victims of these forces' demands for control or influence of editorial content.

News media opacity that hides bribery and other hidden influences and that will be examined in this book is different, however. Because this book examines hidden influences in which sources and news gatherers/disseminators are complicit, and these sources can be multiple, we are collapsing the sources into those whose professional positions include primary responsibility for attempting to place media releases in the news media. These individuals might have a variety of professional titles worldwide, but we will call them public relations practitioners, a label that has a shared meaning that identifies discrete professional communities worldwide.

This book examines the inducements that may be proffered by public relations practitioners who want to influence editorial content, either through rewards, such as bribes, or through punishments, for example, the threat of withdrawal of revenue, as well as the solicitation of these inducements that may be demanded by the news media. Regardless of who initiates these inducements, complicity exists between the sources and the journalists and/or their news media; again, these inducements might be proactively offered to journalists and/or their news media, or journalists and/or their news media might solicit these inducements. An obvious example is a bribe that is offered or solicited as a hidden influence on a gatekeeper's decision to place a media release as editorial content or to provide a preferred place to this media release. Another common example is when the placement of a media release in a newspaper's editorial content is contingent upon advertising that must be bought.

Evidence presented in succeeding chapters of this book suggests that media bribery and other hidden influences occur often and with considerable impunity worldwide. When public relations practitioners pay bribes for their media releases to be disseminated in consumer news media or when other hidden influences alter the information that people consume as "news", a betrayal of trust occurs because journalists and their news media are promoting the illusion among consumers that the news that journalists have gathered and that the news media have disseminated is accurate, complete, and unbiased.

One must ask at this point: Is media opacity that hides bribery and other influences really so problematic, particularly when compared to the other more pronounced and arguably more harmful barriers to truth in the news gathering/disseminating process, for example, the grave physical and psychological threats that journalists face worldwide each day? And should not these hidden influences that are cloaked by news media opacity be assumed, if not tolerated, in cultures that have had long traditions in which these "hidden" influences may at least be transparent abstractly, even if specific examples may be opaque?

These are fair questions that deserve consideration. Apologists for news media bribery and other hidden influences oftentimes cite the need for tolerance because of journalists' low pay in some countries; others will excuse an immature and unsophisticated understanding of the role and function of a free press among sources and journalists and their news media in newly emerging democracies—suggesting the need for patience and forbearance with the assumption that the practice might ultimately disappear on its own as these democracies continue to evolve. Accusations might also be heard concerning a perceived Western hegemony by wealthy and influential public relations agencies and their Western or transnational clients championing Western values. Apologists frequently cite the need for respect for indigenous societies' prevailing social/economic/political traditions as well as for specific cultures' historical antecedents—accompanied with a plea for "cultural sensitivity", together with the need for tolerance and acceptance of well-entrenched indigenous practices.

Indeed, Williams (1995) reminded us that "culture" dictates what constitutes criminality (p. 299). One can easily extend this observation to infer that a pervasive culture also determines what is unethical, albeit perhaps not illegal, within a society. Goodstein, Nolan, and Pfeiffer (1993, p. 58) defined *culture* as a social system based on a central set of beliefs and values. Dicken-Garcia (1989, p. 15) described *values* as the broad dominant social attributes, behaviors, and larger goals that are advocated, promoted, and defended by a society. Goodstein, Nolan, and Pfeiffer (1993, p. 147) said a *value* is an enduring belief that a specific mode of conduct or end-state of existence is personally or socially preferable to an opposite or converse mode of conduct or end-state. Consideration of and respect for a diversity of cultures and values might suggest forbearance of media opacity and the influences that such opacity hides.

However, all of these arguments negate the harm of the lie, as examined in the previous chapter, that is, the violation of trust in which the liar is attempting to mislead the individual being lied to by attempting to create, but then exploit, trust—causing incalculable harm by diminishing the power of the deceived whose choices are altered. People do not like being lied to because they make life decisions based on information that they perceive to be the truth. All of us as citizens and as marketplace consumers want and need *truth*, not *incomplete truth*, or *lies*, from news media that portend to be worthy of *trust*. Also as noted in Chapter 1, our decisions about whom and what to trust become critically important to our well-being as citizens; furthermore, our economic welfare and oftentimes our physical safety as marketplace consumers depend on our determination of what is *truth*, what is an *incomplete truth*, and what is a *lie*. Finally, citizens and marketplace consumers need journalists and their news media whom they can trust because most people have neither the ability nor the time to mine immense amounts of conflicting and oftentimes questionable information from myriad sources to arrive at their own truth.

Thus, apologias for media bribery and other hidden influences that create *incomplete truth* become meaningless when held to the spectrum of what the authors of this book argue is a universal human value, if not right, that is, accurate, complete, and unbiased information that has been gathered and verified conscientiously and competently and that is presented fairly and in good faith by those who are attempting to achieve the ideal of objectivity with complete transparency in gathering, analyzing, and presenting this information. Certainly in no culture or situation can a journalist and his or her consumer news medium ethically declare that they deserve trust when gatekeeping decisions are influenced by factors that are unseen and unknown because of news media opacity. This is especially true in societies that claim to be democratic as well as civil and humane. The authors of this book argue that an attempt to present truth, that is, accurate, complete, and unbiased information that has been gathered and verified conscientiously and competently and that is presented fairly and in good faith by those who are attempting to achieve the ideal of objectivity with complete transparency in gathering, analyzing, and presenting this information must be seen as a universal value and, arguably, a right.

Thus, the authors of this book contend that media bribery and other hidden influences that alter what we consume as "news" can only be regarded as insidious attempts to control people, and these hidden influences must be viewed as a threat to civil society as well as to individuals as citizens and marketplace consumers. Transparency by sources, journalists, and the news media is required to assure that informed citizens and marketplace consumers are given the resources to responsibly and capably make life decisions based on *truth*. The authors conclude that newsworthiness must be the sole criterion that determines presentation as news in a news medium, especially when a media release is to appear in a medium that conveys and reinforces news consumers' implicit assumption that an information subsidy was selected totally because of newsworthiness.

If the Need for Truth and Transparency Exists, Whose Responsibility Is It?

If one accepts these arguments for transparency and against opacity in the news media as compelling, and if one acknowledges the need for truth, rather than incomplete truth, in the news media, whose responsibility is it to assure that news media transparency exists to assure this truth? This is a complex question. The authors of this book argued earlier that the need for news media transparency is universal. However, news media opacity is not universally condemned as being unethical, and it is oftentimes is given tacit acceptance, if not approval. Neither is news media opacity universally illegal, and any laws that might exist may be poorly and erratically enforced or may be given little priority.

Thus, it is best to examine news media opacity that hides incomplete truths as an ethical issue, in particular as a professional ethical issue. One might assume that elimination (or at least the significant reduction) of the practice of media bribery as a hidden influence would be welcomed by public relations practitioners because its elimination would provide obvious economic benefits both to public relations practitioners and to their clients. That is, it reasonably could be assumed these public relations practitioners and their organizations and clients would prefer not to pay bribes that are solicited or demanded by those representing news media to assure the dissemination of media releases that public relations practitioners have provided free-of-charge and that these practitioners feel have intrinsic value to the consumers of news media. That is, public relations practitioners are giving news media a valuable commodity for free, that is, a media release that has inherent value and thus can be sold as a commodity by the news medium for its own profit because of the media release's intrinsic value to the consumers of news. However, one could equally as well assume that at least some public relations practitioners would gladly proffer a bribe to assure placement of a media release that might not otherwise appear in the news media on its own merits. Likewise, journalists and their news media that are seeking trust are certainly free not to solicit bribes and to reject proffered bribes.

Complicity, regardless of the initiation of this complicity, suggests questions of professional ethics for professional communities, that is, public relations practitioners and journalists and their news media. Professional ethics are shaped by two distinct forces: (1) the wider moral principles of a society and (2) the aims of the occupation. These aims will generate functions that, in turn, will generate certain role-based obligations. Ultimately, society's general moral principles provide overall constraints on these aims and functions and how these functions may be executed (Olen, 1988, pp. 5–6). Because of their impact upon society, both public relations practitioners and journalists and their news media have the obligation to act "professionally", that is, socially responsibly, within their indigenous societies, even though they arguably do not fulfill all criteria of a "profession" (Delattre, 1984, p. 12). "Professional" groups develop codes of ethics to define the scope of their membership, identifying who they are as professionals as well as who may join their ranks (Behrman, 1988, p. 104). More importantly, professional groups' codes of ethics also codify these groups' relationship to society (Behrman, 1988, p. 106). Such codes must be consonant with the expectations of society, although—within those confines—society allows professional groups the freedom to determine specifically what they ethically may do in their relationships to society (Behrman, 1988, p. 101). Thus, it is up to the professional group, itself, to define its role within—and responsibility toward—the society in which it practices its profession by defining its own ethics—again, within the moral parameters of that society as well as within the laws of that society's government.

To further confound this ethical issue, one must argue that one professional community does not have the right to dictate the ethics of another professional community that practices within the moral parameters of a society as well as within the laws of that society's government. For example, public relations practitioners as a professional community do not have the right to define the ethics of another professional group, that is, journalists; public relations practitioners as a professional community only have the responsibility to define their own ethical behavior and to enforce it within their own professional community. In the case of media bribery, public relations practitioners have the professional right to declare that they will not proffer media bribes, nor will they yield to demands for media bribes, that is, they will not be willing participants, nor will they allow themselves to become unwilling victims of demands for bribes. Journalists, in turn, are free not to solicit and to reject proffered bribes. Members of a professional community only have the right to control their own behavior, not that of another profession or industry, within the moral parameters of that society as well as within the laws of that society's government.

The Ethical Responsibility as Citizens of Society

The quest for news media transparency and against news media opacity, and the demand for truth, rather than incomplete truth, can only be addressed by the two professional communities, that is, public relations practitioners and journalists and their news media; however, the argument for media transparency and for truth must be made *solely* (and ultimately more compellingly) both by public relations practitioners and journalists and their news media, not as professionals, but rather in their role as citizens—both in their indigenous societies as well as in their role as global citizens whose "professional" values include transparency and truth by public relations practitioners and by journalists and their news media—values that these professionals readily declare as important to society-at-large. Anything less must be viewed as repugnant.

References

Behrman, J. N. (1988). *Essays on ethics in business and the professions*. Englewood Cliffs, NJ: Prentice Hall.

Campbell, R., Martin, C. R., & Fabos, B. (2008). *Media & culture: An introduction to mass communication*. Boston: Bedford/St. Martin's.

Delattre, E. J. (1984). Ethics in the information age. *Public Relations Journal, 40*(6), 12–14.

Dicken-Garcia, H. (1989). *Journalistic standards in nineteenth-century America*. Madison, WI: University of Wisconsin Press.

Goodstein, L., Nolan, T., & Pfeiffer, J. W. (1993). *Applied strategic planning: A comprehensive guide*. New York: McGraw Hill, Inc.

Guralnik, D. B. (Ed.). (1980). *Webster's new world dictionary of the American language* (p. 176). New York: Simon and Schuster.

Hunt, T., & Grunig, J. E. (1994). *Public relations techniques*. Fort Worth, TX: Harcourt Brace College Publishers.

Kruckeberg, D. (1995). International journalism ethics. In J. C. Merrill (Ed.), *Global journalism: Survey of international communication* (pp. 77–87). White Plains, NY: Longman.

Kruckeberg, D., & Tsetsura, K. (2003). International index of bribery for news coverage: A composite index by country of variables related to the likelihood of the existence of "cash for news coverage". *Institute for Public Relations Online: International Research*. Retrieved May 28, 2010 from www.instituteforpr.org/bribery-news-coverage-2003/.

Mencher, M. (2011). *News reporting and writing*. New York: McGraw-Hill.

Merrill, J. C., & Lowenstein, R. L. (1971). *Media, messages, and men: New perspectives in communication*. New York: David McKay Company.

Mundt, W. R. (1991). Global media philosophies. In J. C. Merrill (Ed.), *Global journalism: Survey of international communication*. New York: Longman.

Newsom, D., Turk, J. V., & Kruckeberg, D. (2010). *This is PR: The realities of public relations*. Boston: Wadsworth Cengage Learning.

Olen, J. 1988). *Ethics in journalism*. Englewood Cliffs, NJ: Prentice Hall.

Shoemaker, P. J., Eichholz, M., Kim, E., & Wrigley, B. (2001). Individual and routine forces in gatekeeping. *Journalism & Mass Communication Quarterly*, *78*, 233–246.

Siebert, F., Peterson, T., & Schramm, W. (1956). *Four theories of the press*. Urbana, IL: University of Illinois Press.

Williams, D. E. (1995). Probing cultural implications of war-related victimization in Bosnia-Hercegovina, Croatia, and Serbia. In F. L. Casmir (Ed.), *Communication in Eastern Europe: The role of history, culture, and media in contemporary conflicts* (pp. 277–311). Mahwah, NJ: Lawrence Erlbaum Associates.

3 Media Practice or Media Bribery?
Conceptual and Theoretical Considerations and Implications

- Purpose: The purpose of this chapter is to introduce global theoretical and practical discussions of media practices versus media bribery, highlighting the need for a common denominator when it comes to media transparency worldwide.
- Scope: The practice of purposeful media opacity, which exists to greater or lesser extents worldwide, is a powerful hidden influencer of the ostensibly impartial media gatekeepers whose publicly perceived role is to present news and other information based on these gatekeepers' perception of this information's truthfulness.
- Results: Previous empirical data that the authors have collected globally illustrate the extent of media opacity practices worldwide and note its pervasiveness in specific regions and countries. Using Russian public relations as an example, the authors examine, from multiple perspectives, the complex question of whether media opacity should be categorically condemned as being universally inappropriate and unethical or whether it should be accepted—or at least tolerated—in some situations and environments.
- Conclusions: It is essential to continue promoting ethical practices for educational and professional communities in the name of a better future of global media transparency. This is an ultimate challenge in combating media opacity worldwide.

In today's global society, in which the compression of time and space has resulted in increased social-political-economic-cultural complexity worldwide, most of what we accept to be truth comes from the myriad forms of "mass media", for example, the newspapers that we read, the television programs that we watch, the radio stations to which we listen and the infinite Internet sources that we explore. We rely—most often by necessity—upon these secondary sources to help us to determine our own truths that create our unique worldviews from which we form our individual beliefs, attitudes, and opinions that directly influence the decisions that we make.

This chapter is about media transparency and good-faith attempts of honesty by both the sources and the gatekeepers of news and other information that the mass media present as being unbiased. Specifically, we discuss conceptual considerations for understanding media transparency and its antithesis—media opacity—throughout the world. The practice of purposeful media opacity, which exists to greater or lesser extents worldwide, is a powerful hidden influencer of the ostensibly impartial media gatekeepers whose publicly perceived role is to present news and other information based on these gatekeepers' perception of this information's truthfulness. Empirical data that the authors have collected globally illustrate the extent of media opacity practices worldwide and note its pervasiveness in specific regions and countries (Kruckeberg & Tsetsura, 2003). Media opacity creates difficulty accessing truth.

Truth is essential in democratic societies, but again what is truth? Those in democratic nation-states require not only the right to express public opinion, but to form public opinion that is based on unbiased news and information and impartial gatekeepers from transparent media from which this public opinion can be informed. Much as fairness and balance are often achieved in the pursuit of the ideal of an unattainable objectivity, the chapter argues that transparency and honesty can be achieved in the pursuit of an ideal truth.

In this chapter, we view truth through unique lenses and from multiple sources. Each individual's worldview is comprised of an infinite number of variables that have uniquely molded each of us to be the individuals that we are, and this worldview provides the foundation from which each of us must form our own unique perceptions of truth. While we may have multiple resources to seek truth, sampling sources for truth becomes problematic because of the purposeful hidden influences of media opacity. Truth can be seen through each individual's unique lens and can be influenced by sole sources and multiple sources as well as by unreliable sources and ostensibly reliable sources. Should truth be regulated? If so, by whom? Media opacity resulting from purposeful hidden influencers of what is presented is what distinguishes purposeful opacity from simple opacity, when opacity could have been a simple act of misunderstanding or a result of ignorance of social and cultural norms and practices.

Mass media as secondary sources are relied upon to form our beliefs, attitudes, and opinions from which each of us arrives at his or her unique truth that forms within the context of each individual's worldview. The disintegration of the concept of news and the increasingly amorphous role of the journalist are examined, that is, what a contemporary journalist is and should be, today's distinction between controlled vs. uncontrolled media, and the role of the journalist as an arbiter and a representative and protector of the disenfranchised and powerless. And, in today's world, the public relations practitioner has a new critical role in presenting truth to the media as well as to society at large.

Media Practice or Media Opacity?

The practice of purposeful media opacity, which exists to greater or lesser extents worldwide, is a powerful hidden influencer of the ostensibly impartial media gatekeepers whose publicly perceived role is to present news and other information based on these gatekeepers' perception of this information's truthfulness. Previous empirical data that the authors have collected globally illustrate the extent of media opacity practices worldwide and note its pervasiveness in specific regions and countries. This conceptual chapter examines a complex question of whether media opacity should be categorically condemned as being universally inappropriate and unethical or whether it should be accepted—or at least tolerated—in some situations and environments.

Who can evaluate what media opacity is? Public relations practitioners and their clients may have an economic incentive to eliminate purposeful media opacity, but their concern must be secondary to all citizens' greater concerns about the social ills that are created by bribes paid to media workers, for example. A dynamic marketplace of ideas to sustain and encourage democratic societies and free marketplace economies requires the integrity of communication channels, particularly of consumer news media that are ostensibly "fair" and "balanced" in their quest for the ideal of "objectivity". Nevertheless, compelling arguments for the elimination of news media opacity for the placement of information subsidies, as an example, must satisfactorily address several issues.

For example, apologists for the practice will cite the need for tolerance because of journalists' subsistence or low pay in some countries; others will note an immature and unsophisticated understanding of the role and function of a free press among those in newly emerging democracies—suggesting the need for patience and forbearance because the practice might ultimately disappear on its own as these democracies continue to evolve. Accusations might also be heard concerning perceived Western hegemony through the influence of public relations agencies and their clients, perhaps accompanied by a plea for "cultural sensitivity". Cited also are indigenous societies' prevailing social/economic/political climates as well as specific cultures' historical antecedents, again accompanied with a plea for tolerance and acceptance of indigenous practices. Finally, some may say that what is called opacity in one country might be accepted protocol in another.

Such arguments can be easily refuted; however, defenders of consumer news media opacity are essentially correct that public relations practitioners cannot as a professional group impose and declare valid their professional culture and values upon another professional group, that is, upon journalists and other mass media workers, nor do the latter have the right to impose their values upon public relations practitioners. It can be argued that, as communication professionals, public relations practitioners and journalists only have the right to control their own professional/occupational behavior, not that of other professional communities, nor does this professional community have the moral right to censure or criticize the ethics of the news media for which journalists work.

Rather, the argument against purposeful mass media opacity by those providing or accepting information subsidies must be made solely (and ultimately more compellingly) by public relations practitioners and news media workers, for example, journalists, in their mutual role as citizens of the countries in which purposeful news media opacity occurs—but also as global citizens whose values must include truth and honesty in message construction and dissemination worldwide. Most definitely, public relations practitioners and journalists *do* have the professional right and obligation to declare what they consider to be ethical and unethical for their own discrete professional communities. For instance, if a professional group of journalists in one country agrees that a given practice is ethical and professional in their professional community, and if this behavior is within the parameters of the law, then purposeful opacity within that cultural context is both acceptable and, to that extent, transparent. Of course, if journalists in a country believe this is an ethically acceptable professional practice, this would mean that their understanding of professionalism in relation to journalism would be different from the predominant Western perspective on journalism. However, if a group of journalists (or public relations practitioners) in one country believes that this is a practice that does not adhere to ethical standards of the profession in that country, even though it routinely occurs in practice, that means this is a concern for professionals in that country. Such a practice, if continued, can diminish the status and ethics of the profession. As such, this phenomenon should be voiced and discussed as one of the central issues and challenges that can damage the profession throughout the world.

We argue that it is important to distinguish between news media non-transparency and purposeful media opacity because transparency is first and foremost a requirement for credible media practices that are based on trust between the media representatives and their audiences. But what influencers should be transparent, and what should be disclosed? Must media transparency and media opacity be understood or regarded differently in different parts of the world, or should universal standards apply? A good way to answer this question is to take a look at the practices of media opacity in two completely different media environments. For the purpose of this argument, the authors chose examples from the USA, Russia, and several other countries to illustrate how the discourse about media non-transparency transforms into the discourse about purposeful media opacity with time.

Media Transparency vs. Media Opacity

Media transparency is a building block for professional news media development based on trust between the media and the audience (Tsetsura & Kruckeberg, 2009). Journalists must be open and thus transparent with their audiences (Kovach, 2001). Honesty, independence of opinion, fair judgment, and traditional news values are the main factors that define journalistic principles and define news media credibility. If one or several of these principles are violated, the audience has a right to know what influenced journalistic decisions (Craig, 1999, 2006, 2008). The absence of any direct and indirect influence is central to the concept of media transparency. Lack of disclosure of influences and constraints placed on journalists, editors, and the media in which articles or programs appear is often referred to as non-transparency (Tsetsura & Grynko, 2009). Publishing news in exchange for a payment or a favor compromises a traditional function of mass media in society and undermines media's roles as gatekeepers (Boynton, 2007; Craig, 2007; Pasti, 2005).

Non-transparent practices can be found worldwide (Tsetsura & Kruckeberg, 2009). Understanding how diverse information sources, such as public relations practitioners who work for organizations, can influence the news is at heart of media non-transparency studies (Tsetsura & Kruckeberg, 2009; Tsetsura & Grynko, 2009; Klyueva, 2008). The growing amount of research on the topic (Kruckeberg & Tsetsura, 2003; Tsetsura, 2005a, 2005b; Klyueva, 2008; Tsetsura & Grynko, 2009) defined the phenomenon of media non-transparency as any form of payment for or influence on news coverage. News media non-transparency has also been known as cash for news coverage (Kruckeberg & Tsetsura, 2003), media bribery (Tsetsura, 2005b), envelope journalism (Shafer, 1990), paid news (Tsetsura, 2015), and media opacity (Tsetsura & Kruckeberg, 2009). Many practitioners around the world also use slang words to refer to this phenomenon: *zakazukha* in Russia (Holmes, 2001), *jinsa* in Ukraine (Tsetsura & Grynko, 2009), *mermelada* in Peru (Ristow, 2010), and *pay-for-play* in the USA (Tsetsura, 2008). The authors of this book argue that media opacity is the most accurate concept to describe such a practice because it communicates a deliberative effort to influence an editor's or journalist's decision to purposefully hide a source of information or influence.

Once again as an analogy, *transparency* exists in a lighted room, but *opacity* occurs when the lights are turned off and darkness results. What can be seen in the light is hidden in darkness. Perhaps the darkness hides nothing, but it certainly can hide a lot. Turning the lights off and thus bringing darkness into the room (purposeful opacity) creates a perfect condition for violating established or ostensible rules and norms. If someone punches you in a dark room, you may or may not know who has done it. Darkness hides the one who had punched you, and thus that individual does not have to explain why he or she has done it. This purposeful punch that has no consequences is only possible in the darkness. The same is true for media opacity because a purposeful non-disclosure of influences on the news allows non-transparent media practices, including, but not limited to, direct and indirect payments to the media from news sources, pressure from advertising departments, and financial pressure on the media.

Understanding Media Opacity

The problem of credibility in the media lies at the essence of independent, objective, and responsible journalism. But what exactly encompasses this objectivity and how independent can today's media, self-supported by advertiser's money in some countries and subsidized by the governments in others, be? And what role does journalism integrity play in the modern world of materialism? In the investigative report "Money vs. Ethics: A Balancing Act" published in 2003, International Press Institute journalist Mike McGraw tried to answer these difficult, but important, questions. He provided specific examples of how media professionals can discredit themselves by accepting bribes from information sources. He demonstrated that media bribery has become one of the most difficult problems to overcome. Editors, reporters, and specialized journalists are dependent on sources to provide accurate, up-to-date, relevant information that becomes the basis for news. This information is fast, detailed, and current in the modern information era. Most importantly, this information comes for free. Journalists do not need to personally search for and gather information any longer; they often only need to perform their gatekeeping role of deciding whether to distribute this information through media channels and thus set the news agenda. And we, as a public, rely on journalists to decide which information is the most important, most newsworthy, and most relevant for us from the constant huge flow of information.

As such, we expect the news media to follow several essential information gatekeeping principles: independence of opinion, fair and honest judging of facts and reporting, and freedom and autonomy from outside, non-media influences. Most importantly, we expect media workers to separate for us on the pages of newspapers and magazines and on the air space of radio and TV programming what materials are truly journalistic news-editorial content and what materials are advertising, such as paid-for publication by sources of information. This is what we call a sense of ethical behavior. A special case of media opacity has been at the center of debates on the nature of publicity materials and media relations practices for a long time. Offering and paying cash for publishing publicity materials, news releases, and other content often becomes the norm and a standard practice in many countries (Kruckeberg & Tsetsura, 2003).

Media opacity is defined as a favorable condition for any form of payment for news coverage or any influence on editors and journalists' decisions that is not clearly stated in the finished journalistic product. Media opacity takes place in many countries (Kruckeberg & Tsetsura, 2003; Tsetsura & Grynko, 2009; Tsetsura & Kruckeberg, 2009). Research showed that media opacity is a serious problem in the Eastern European counties, including Estonia, Poland, China, Russia, and Ukraine (Tsetsura, 2005b; Pasti, 2005; Harro-Loit & Saks, 2006; Klyueva, 2008; Tsetsura & Grynko, 2009; Tsetsura & Klyueva, 2010; Tsetsura, 2015). Previous multiple studies showed that paying cash for news coverage, placing advertising in the media in exchange for news coverage, as well as providing gifts, free meals, or free trips to journalists and editors in exchange for publications in which real sources of influence are not disclosed are practices that are present in much of the world. In most of the world, however, this practice of media opacity is condemned by both professional groups: public relations practitioners and journalists (Tsetsura, 2008).

Some critics have advocated that such media practices are part of the culture in some places around the world, but no studies have shown that culture has influenced the decision-making processes of journalists and public relations practitioners in the case of media opacity. Professionals in some regions of the world emphasized that direct or indirect influences on the media are common practices in countries such as China and Russia (Tsetsura, 2015; Tsetsura & Luoma-aho, 2010). But almost 85 percent of the professionals who are members of international organizations, including the International Public Relations Association, International Press Institute, and International Federation of Journalists, from throughout the world condemn these practices as unprofessional and unethical (Tsetsura, 2008). Additional multi-year research of global media practices have convincingly demonstrated that culture is not a factor that predicts these differences (Kruckeberg & Tsetsura, 2003; Klyueva, 2008; Tsetsura & Grynko, 2009; Klyueva & Tsetsura, 2010). Explaining these practices simply as a result of cultural differences might be a simplistic and somewhat naïve way of understanding and analyzing the problem. Rather than dismissing these practices as a cultural particularity, political, economic, historical, and societal factors, as well as the level of professional development and practice and the development of ethical conduct, should be taken into consideration when one attempts to define whether media relations practices in a certain country are perceived as corrupt or unethical. The next section illustrates how political historical, economical, and societal factors have been manifested throughout the history of journalism in Russia and how this history has influenced, and continues to influence, media opacity in the modern practice of Russian public relations.

The Influence of Journalism on the Development of Public Relations in Russia

Understanding the history of journalism in Russia is essential for knowing how media practices have developed in this country. Traditionally, freedom of the press has not been the first and foremost right of Russian citizens (McReynolds, 1991). The very first newspaper in Russia, *"Sankt-Peterburgskie vedomosti"* [Saint Petersburg Gazette], started by the order of tsar Peter the Great, was transferred to the control of the state-run Academy of Sciences in 1703 (Zassoursky, 2004). Because of political and economic changes, post-Soviet Russian journalism has undergone several crucial changes, but the challenges that journalism faced were still very much a part of the historical baggage (Ragozina, 2007). The post-Soviet media system, with a strong emphasis on economic independence and market orientation, contributed to the development of public relations in Russia. The origins of Russian public relations are in journalism as the very first public relations practitioners were journalists (Tsetsura, 2003), and Russian public relations theory and practice are built on journalistic traditions (Tsetsura, 2004).

Each of the three major periods into which the history of Russian journalism can be divided has contributed to the unique development of journalism and public relations in Russia (Cassara, Gross, Kruckeberg, Palmer, & Tsetsura, 2004). The first period is the pre-Soviet period from the eighteenth to the early twentieth centuries; the Soviet period covers 1917–1985, which includes the development of the Soviet function of journalism and the beginning of the *perestroika* period; and finally, the Gorbachev and post-Soviet period covers 1985–2000, during which there was free speech without regulation, rules, or restrictions (Klyueva & Tsetsura, 2011). Recently, a new period was identified as the Putin Era period, which covers the development of journalism from 2000 until the present time (Koltsova, 2006).

When Bolsheviks came to power in 1917, a state monopoly on advertising was installed to deprive the commercial press of its main source of income.

The young Soviet government believed that a truly free press can only be formed without any capitalistic or market-driven principles and influences (Koltsova, 2006). But soon, the Soviet period of journalism was characterized by a combination of an extreme media control and censorship and little attention to public opinion about the media (Koltsova, 2006). During the Soviet era, mass media were treated as means of mass information and propaganda, and the media's function was to report the government news and to propagate socialist ideals (McNair, 1991).

A true rebirth of the principles of objectivity and openness in journalism happened when Gorbachev initiated a *Glasnost* campaign in 1984. The new information policy established principles of freedom of information, pluralism of opinions, and open exchange of ideas among citizens (Zhirkov, 2001). Economic and political reforms led to a free market economy and opened doors to the development of all market-driven industries, including advertising, marketing, and public relations (Tsetsura, 2004). Journalists were the first people in Russia who started working in the field of public relations. The first and foremost function of these new public relations practitioners was to deliver information to the mass media, similar to the Western tradition of media relations (Goregin & Nikolaev, 1996). And, because these journalists knew how the media system worked in Russia, they were the best professionals for this new job.

As the markets developed in Russia, the concerns with corporate ownership and the commercialization of journalism became inevitable. Pasti (2005) argued that journalists of the 1990s perceived journalism as a handy public relations tool that could benefit influential groups, rather than an objective profession, that is, an independent entity that serves society. Harro-Loit and Saks (2006) demonstrated that the commercialization of journalism led to blurred borders between journalism and advertising in Eastern Europe. Continuing commercialization and economic pressures led to a re-conceptualization of public relations and journalism in Russia and to the rapid development of media opacity. Are there any additional factors that can help one to understand why in certain countries, particularly in Russia, media opacity is so widely spread? To answer this question, one should take a closer look at the development of public relations as a field in Russia and should examine the phenomenon of "black" vs. "white" Russian public relations.

Media Opacity in Russian Public Relations

The two terms "black PR" and "white PR" were first introduced in the late 1980s and early 1990s and soon became very popular among professionals and scholars in Russia (Tsetsura, 2003). According to the "black vs. white PR" view, ethics divide public relations practices into "black" and "white", or "bad and good". "Black PR" is associated with manipulative techniques that were often used in political public relations and political election campaigns (Tsetsura, 2003). Essentially, "black PR" emerged as another term for media opacity in Russian political public relations. "White PR", on the other hand, presented a Western view of public relations, which is rooted in the ethical Grunig's *Excellence Project* (Maksimov, 1999). In many discussions about public relations practices in Russia, public relations scholars, practitioners, and journalists often refer to the field in terms of "black" and "white".

Some scholars disagree that public relations practices should be described as "black and white" (Klyueva & Tsetsura, 2011). Instead of categorizing public relations as "black" or "white", they argue that "black" public relations is not public relations at all, but rather propagandistic efforts (Tsetsura, 2003). They gleaned that "black vs. white PR" discussions take place because the profession has been slow to adopt ethical standards (Tsetsura & Grynko, 2009). Some U.S. scholars argued that "black" public relations cannot exist because "any misuse or abuse of public relations is a question, not of 'bad' public relations of which only an individual practitioner can be held responsible, but rather such misuse or abuse becomes a question of unethical professional practice which is of collective concern and which must be collective responsibility of all practitioners" (Kruckeberg, 1992, p. 34).

From a Western perspective, public relations professional ethics is not followed in Russia. Russian professionals have joined associations (for example, the International Public Relations Association (IPRA), International Association of Business Communicators (IABC), and the Public Relations Society of America (PRSA), and subscribed to follow those organizations' codes of ethics. However, many of them find these rules and codes to be idealistic and not well-suited for the Russian public relations environment (Tsetsura, 2003). The main problem, however, lies in the fact that these Russian professionals, themselves, actively argue for ethical public relations in their everyday discourses and agree that they do not act ethically when they break public relations codes of ethics (Klyueva, 2008; Pashentsev, 2002). Thus, the argument that Russian public relations ethics is not the same as Western ethics becomes questionable: If Russian public relations practitioners agree that, for instance, publishing press releases for money is wrong (Klyueva & Tsetsura, 2011), how can this practice be ethical in the eyes of Russian public relations practitioners?

Many Russian public relations scholars and practitioners are concerned with an existing practice of paying money to journalists and editors for publishing publicity materials (Klyueva & Tsetsura, 2011; Tsetsura & Luoma-aho, 2010). While such instances originally took place in Moscow and St. Petersburg, now the problem is becoming more and more common in many other regions in Russia. This practice is often called "zakazukha", a Russian slang word which means material in favor of an organization written by a journalist and published on editorial pages, but paid for by that organization to a journalist or an editor. In a classic experiment, Promaco Public Relations, a Moscow-based public relations firm, showed that 13 out of 21 Russian national newspapers and magazines were ready to publish a fake press release (without even checking the facts), charging from $200 to $2000 for the service (Sutherland, 2001). According to Russian laws, this unlawful activity is called hidden advertising. Unfortunately, a law against hidden advertising, which periodically appears in the Russian media, is not enforced. Journalists who get paid, or public relations professionals who pay for materials to be published, are not legally challenged for their wrongdoings. As a result of such non-enforcement of punishment, media opacity became a standard practice in the early days of Russian public relations (Tsetsura, 2011). That created a strong negative perception of the field from the very start and to this day affects the credibility of the professional public relations practices (Tsetsura, 2003).

Media Opacity in Other Countries

Examples of media opacity from Russia played a significant role in attracting the public's attention to this worldwide problem, and the phenomenon was publicly discussed at several international conferences of professionals in public relations and journalism. Many agreed that examples from Moscow are probably extreme cases since often it is called a "bribery capital", but Vuslat Doğan Sabanci, CEO of Hürriyet, Doğan Media Group, confirmed that anecdotal evidence of zakazukha exists in many other countries (Ovaitt, 2004). Examples of media bribery can be found around the world. Media bribery in Egypt was reported in *The Economist* (Gamal, the brisk new broom: Egypt's political scandals, 2002, Sept. 7) when Muhammad Wakil, a director of news for Egypt's state television monopoly, was caught for taking a bribe to put a doctor on a popular talk show. As the investigation showed, Wakil had been charging "clients" for years to appear on popular shows. The United Kingdom specialists often report that the trade magazines ask for "color separations" payments when they use a company's photo on their pages. No one argues that certain make-up brands are chosen for the front cover of many beauty magazines because those brands are the biggest advertisers in the corresponded media.

One media opacity scandal in the USA involved the well-known Ketchum PR agency and the Bush administration. Ketchum had received a contract to promote the No Child Left Behind (NCLB) campaign, an educational campaign actively advocated by the Republican administration. It turned out that Armstrong Williams, a famous TV commentator, entrepreneur, and founder of an advertising/PR firm, who actively supported the education campaign and often discussed it in a favorable light in his programs on the American TV channels, was a subcontractor for Ketchum. His job, according to the contract, was to actively promote the campaign's benefits and advantages.

When the scandal broke out in the middle of January 2005, Mr. Williams issued an apology: "Please know that I supported school vouchers long before the Department of Education ran a single ad on my TV Show. I did not change my views just because my PR firm was receiving paid advertising promoting the No Child Left Behind" (Williams, 2005). He continued, "I now realize that I have to create inseparable boundaries between my role as a small businessman and my role as an independent commentator (Williams, 2005). It seems, at the very least, strange to hear a comment like this one from an experienced public relations professional and, more importantly, from a famous journalist who finally realized that he had needed to create boundaries between the two roles.

The reaction from competitors was furious: Richard Edelman, president of Edelman PR, said, "This kind of pay for play public relations takes us back in time to the days of the press agent who would drop off the new record album and $10 to the deejay" (Edelman, 2005). Ketchum's response shortly followed, and Ray Kotcher, CEO of Ketchum PR, said the agency regretted the lack of disclosure. "We should have recognized the potential issues in working with a communications firm operated by a commentator", the statement said. "This work did not comply with the guidelines of our agency and our industry" (Elliott, 2005). The client, the Department of Education, also reacted to the scandal, with Education Secretary Margaret Spellings stating, "At this point, what I can say is that at a minimum, there were errors of judgment at the Department, and I am diligently working to get to the bottom of it all" (Toppo, 2005).

But despite the international attention and the fact that the global professional community condemns this practice, to this day, some practitioners, specifically those who practice public relations in some regions of the world, readily admit that they do not always practice ethical public relations as presented in the code of ethics of their respective professional public relations associations, such as RASO, a Russian public relations association. Russian practitioners, for instance, argue that common perceptions of "black PR" and widespread bribery make it difficult to practice Western-style, "white" public relations (Pashentsev, 2002; Tsetsura, 2003). Some simply say that it is impossible to practice ethical public relations because nobody pays for ethics (Maksimov, 1999). But these excuses are weak for two reasons: (1) the majority of the practitioners throughout the world do agree that ethics need to be taken into consideration while practicing public relations, particularly in regard to media transparency (Klyueva & Tsetsura, 2011; Tsetsura & Grynko, 2009; Tsetsura, 2015); and (2) scholars and practitioners throughout the world actively defend the principles of public relations codes of ethics as a unifying element of international public relations (Alyoshina, 1997; Bowen, 2008; Bowen, Rawlins, & Martin, 2010; Boynton, 2007; Egorova, 2000; Klyueva & Tsetsura, 2010; Konovalova, 2000; Lebedeva, 1999; Pashentsev, 2002; Tsetsura, 2008; Tsetsura & Kruckeberg, 2004).

Conclusion

Public relations professional organizations as well as practitioners throughout the world face the same problem as those in Russia: accepted codes of ethics are not enforceable and thus are not practiced (Tsetsura & Grynko, 2009; Tsetsura, 2015). Although codes of ethics exist worldwide, specialists point out numerous problems with their reinforcement. One of the goals of public relations practitioners and educators is to find better ways to reinforce such codes and position benefits for following these codes. This goal can be quite challenging, especially for modern public relations practitioners who work in different countries; however, it is critically important to continue promoting ethical practices for educational and professional communities in the name of a better future for global public relations. And this is an ultimate challenge in combating media opacity worldwide.

References

Alyoshina, I. (1997). *Public relations dlja menedgerov i marketerov* [Public relations for managers and marketers]. Moscow, RU: Gnom-press.

Bowen, S. A. (2008). A state of neglect: Public relations as corporate conscience or ethics counsel. *Journal of Public Relations Research, 20,* 271–296.

Bowen, S., Rawlins, B., & Martin. T. (2010). *An overview of the public relations function.* Williston, VT: Business Expert Press.

Boynton, L. A. (2007). Commentaries: Commentary 1: This PR firm should have known better. *Journal of Mass Media Ethics, 22,* 218–221.

Cassara, C., Gross, P., Kruckeberg, D., Palmer, A., & Tsetsura, K. (2004). Eastern Europe, the newly independent states of Eurasia, and Russia. In A.S. de Beer & J. C. Merrill (Eds.), *Global journalism: Topical issues and media systems* (pp. 212–256). Boston: Pearson.

Craig, D. A. (2008). Journalists, government, and the place of journalism across cultures. *Journal of Mass Media Ethics, 23,* 158–161.

Craig, D. A. (2007). The case: Wal-Mart public relations in the blogosphere. *Journal of Mass Media Ethics, 22,* 215–228.

Craig, D. A. (2006). *The ethics of the story: Using narrative techniques responsibility in journalism.* Lanham, MD: Rowman & Littlefield.

Craig, D. A. (1999). A framework for evaluating coverage of ethics in professions and society. *Journal of Mass Media Ethics, 14,* 16–27.

Edelman, R. (2005, January 7). Pay to play PR is not on. *6 A.M.* Retrieved from www.edelman.com/p/6-a-m/pay-to-play-pr-is-not-on/.

Egorova, A. (2000). *International public relations: Order out of chaos. A Delphi study focusing on Russia.* Unpublished master's thesis, University of Lousiana, Lafayette.

Elliott, S. (2005, January 20). Agency admits errors in deal with TV host. *New York Times* Retrieved from www.nytimes.com/2005/01/20/business/media/agency-admits-errors-in-deal-with-tv-host.html.

Gamal, the brisk new broom: Egypt's political scandals (2002, Sept. 7). *The Economist,* 364, pp. 61. Retrieved from www.economist.com/node/1316901.

Goregin, A. G., & Nikolaev, A. G. (1996). Evolution of modern Russian communication. *Communication World, 13,* 68–70.

Harro-Loit, H., & Saks, K. (2006). The diminishing border between advertising and journalism in Estonia. *Journalism Studies, 7,* 312–322.

Holmes, P. (2001, March 5). Russian PR firm exposes media corruption. *The Holmes Report. 1*(9). Retrieved from www.holmesreport.com/story.cfm?edit_id=156&typeid=1.

Klyueva, A. (2008). *An exploratory study of media transparency in the Urals Federal District of Russia.* Unpublished master's thesis, University of Oklahoma, Norman, OK.

Klyueva, A., & Tsetsura, K. (2011). News from the Urals with love and payment: The first look at non-transparent media practices in the Urals Federal District of Russia. *Russian Journal of Communication, 4*(1/2), 72–93.

Klyueva, A., & Tsetsura, K. (2010, March). *Ethicality of media opacity as a predictor of acceptance of non-transparent media practices among the Romanian media professionals.* Paper presented at the 13th IPR International Public Relations Research conference, Miami, FL.

Koltsova, O. (2006). *News media and power in Russia.* London; New York: Routledge.

Konovalova, E. (2000, April). A za PR otvetish' pered … sovest'ju [You will be responsible for PR with your own dignity]. Electronic version of magazine *Sovetnik.* Retrieved from www.sovetnik.ru/archive/2000/4/article.asp?id=2.

Kovach, B. (2001). *Elements of journalism: What newspeople should know and the public should expect.* Westminster, MD, USA: Crown Publishing Group, Incorporated.

Kruckeberg, D. (1992). Ethical decision-making in public relations. *International Public Relations Review, 15,* 32–37.

Kruckeberg, D., & Tsetsura, K. (2003). *International index of bribery for news coverage.* Institute for Public Relations. Retrieved from www.instituteforpr.org/bribery-news-coverage-2003/.

Lebedeva, T. Y. (1999). *Public relations. Korporativnaya i politicheskaya rezhissura* [Public relations: Corporate and political directing]. Moskva: MGU.

Maksimov, A. A. (1999). *"Chistye" i "gryaznye" teknologii vyborov: Rossijskij opyt* ["Clean" and "dirty" technologies of political elections: Russian experience]. Moscow, RU: Delo.

McGraw, M. (2003, April 1). Money vs. Ethics: A balancing act. IPI Global Journalist. Retrieved from http://globaljournalist.jour.missouri.edu/stories/2003/04/01/money-vs-ethics/.

McNair, B. (1991). *Glasnost, perestroika, and the Soviet media.* London: Routledge.

McReynolds, L. (1991). *The news under Russia's old regime: The development of a mass- circulation press.* Princeton, NJ: Princeton University Press.

Ovaitt, F. (2004). Putting an end to bribery for news coverage. In International Press Institute (Ed.), *IPI Congress Report: Warsaw 2004* (pp. 67–68). Vienna, Austria. International Press Institute (IPI). Retrieved from http://ipi.freemedia.at/fileadmin/resources/application/2004_IPI_Warsaw_Congress_Report.pdf.

Pashentsev, E. N. (2002). *Public relations: Ot biznesa do politiki, 3 izdanie* [Public relations: From business to politics, 3rd edition]. Moskva, RU: Finpress.

Pasti, S. (2005). Two generations of contemporary Russian journalists. *European Journal of Communication, 20,* 89–114.

Ragozina, I. (2007). *The status of public relations in Russia.* Unpublished master's thesis, East Tennessee State University, Johnson City, TN.

Ristow, B. (2010). *Cash for coverage: Bribery of journalists around the world.* A Report to the Center for International Media Assistance. Electronic version. Retrieved from http://cima.ned.org/sites/default/files/CIMA-Bribery_of_Journalists-Report.pdf.

Shafer, R. (1990). Greasing the newsgate: Journalist on the take in the Philippines. *Journal of Mass Media Ethics, 5,* 15–29.

Sutherland, A. (2001). PR thrives in harder times. *Frontline, IPRA, 23,* 5.

Toppo, G. (2005, January 30). Spellings: "Errors of judgment" made in paying Williams. *USA Today.* Retrieved from http://usatoday30.usatoday.com/news/washington/2005-01-30-spellings-williams_x.htm.

Tsetsura, K. (2015). Guanxi, gift-giving, or bribery? Ethical considerations of paid news in China. *Public Relations Journal, 9*(2). Retrieved from www.prsa.org/Intelligence/PRJournal/Documents/2015v09n02Tsetsura.pdf.

Tsetsura, K. (2011). Cultural and historical aspects of media transparency in Russia. In A. G. Nikolaev (Ed.), *Ethics issues in international communication* (pp. 172–182). New York: Palgrave Macmillan.

Tsetsura, K. (2008). An exploratory study of global media relations practices. *Institute for Public Relations Research Reports: International Research.* Retrieved from www.instituteforpr.com/international.phtml.

Tsetsura, K. (2005a). *The exploratory study of media transparency and cash for news coverage practice in Russia: Evidence from Moscow PR agencies.* Proceedings of the 8th International Interdisciplinary public relations research conference, Miami, FL: University of Miami.

Tsetsura, K. (2005b). Bribery for news coverage: Research in Poland (peer-reviewed research article). *Institute for Public Relations Online: International Research.* Retrieved from www.instituteforpr.com/international.phtml.

Tsetsura, K. (2004). Russia. In B. van Ruler & D. Vercic (Eds.), *Public relations and communication management in Europe: A nation-by-nation introduction to public relations theory and practice* (pp. 331–346). Berlin: Mouton de Gruyter.

Tsetsura, K. (2003). The development of public relations in Russia: A geopolitical approach. In K. Sriramesh, & D. Vercic (Eds.), *A handbook of international public relations* (pp. 301–319). Mahwah, NJ: Lawrence Erlbaum Assoc. Inc.

Tsetsura, K., & Grynko, A. (2009). An exploratory study of media transparency in Ukraine. *Public Relations Journal, 3*(2). Retrieved from www.prsa.org/prjournal/index.html?WT.ac=PRJournalTopNav.

Tsetsura, K., & Klyueva, A. (2010). Ethicality of media opacity as a predictor of acceptance of non-transparent media practices among the Romanian media professionals. *Proceedings of the 13th international interdisciplinary public relations research conference* (p. 696). Miami, FL: University of Miami. Retrieved from www.instituteforpr.org/wp-content/uploads/IPRRC_13_Proceedings.pdf.

Tsetsura, K., & Kruckeberg, D. (2009). Truth, public relations and the mass media: A normative model to examine media opacity. *Proceedings of the 12th international interdisciplinary public relations research conference*, Miami, FL: University of Miami.

Tsetsura, K., & Kruckeberg, D. (2004). Theoretical development of public relations in Russia. In D. J. Tilson (Ed.), *Toward the common good: Perspectives in international public relations* (pp. 176–192). Boston: Pearson Allyn & Bacon.

Tsetsura, K., & Luoma-aho, V. (2010). Innovative thinking or distortion of journalistic values? How the lack of trust creates non-transparency in the Russian media. *Ethical Space: The International Journal of Communication Ethics, 7*, 30–38.

Williams, A. (2005, January). My apology. Retrieved from www.beliefnet.com/News/2005/01/My-Apology.aspx.

Zassoursky, I. (2004) *Media and power in post-Soviet Russia*. New York: M.E. Sharpe.

Zhirkov, G. V. (2001).*Istoriya cenzuri v Rossii v IXX –XX veka* [History of censorship in Russia in 19th–20th centuries]. Moscow, RU: Aspect-Press.

4   Dispelling the Myths of the Ethical Significance and Validity of the Concept of Cultural Relativism and the Need for Cultural Tolerance in Combatting Media Bribery Worldwide

- Purpose: In calling for truth through transparency in the news media worldwide, to dispel the myths of (1) the relevance and ethical significance and validity of the concept of cultural relativism and (2) the need for cultural tolerance.
- Scope: To argue for the global relevance and universal applicability of the arguments and recommendations in this book.
- Method: To frame the need for media transparency as an obvious, albeit complex, ethical issue to which a moral consensus is nevertheless unlikely because of disparate ethical perspectives worldwide and because hidden influences of journalists and their news media, which are made possible through media opacity, are highly profitable and advantageous to some journalists, their news media, and public relations practitioners, which influences are often either unknown or tacitly accepted by citizens and marketplace consumers; rather, the need for media transparency is more likely to become universally accepted as a norm, or at least more highly valued, by framing news media transparency through arguments that are predicated on the premise that truth resulting from media transparency has both economic and intrinsic value and can be marketed effectively through branding.
- Results: The reader will accept the authors' arguments about the economic and intrinsic value of truth in considering the need for media transparency and in the rejection of media opacity; news media will conclude that, through transparency that eliminates hidden influences, journalists and their news media will add economic and intrinsic value to their product, news, by distinguishing their product from the incomplete truths that result from hidden influences; and consumers of news will value truth resulting from media transparency because they will perceive and appreciate its enhanced economic and intrinsic value.
- Recommendations: The reader should ponder the problem of news media opacity that allows hidden influences that create incomplete

truths, and the reader is encouraged to consider and to accept the thesis of this book. Furthermore, the global community of professional journalists, their news media, and the global community of public relations practitioners should declare that hidden influences that are cloaked by media opacity are categorically professionally unethical.

- Conclusions: Media transparency should be a universal ethical norm, and news media opacity that allows hidden influences should be recognized as professionally unethical, but global consensus about the desirability of media transparency is unlikely; however, media transparency that eliminates hidden influences can be framed and marketed universally through branding based on the economic and intrinsic value of truth.

Citizens Will Need to Rely on Journalists They Can Trust

In Chapter 1, we argued that journalists in their professional role and news media as a societal institution will remain unequivocally important in twenty-first-century global society, albeit largely for different reasons than in the past; indeed, journalists and their news media will be essential in safeguarding us (1) as citizens, both in our indigenous nation-states as well as worldwide and (2) as consumers in the global marketplace. Rapid and immense changes in communication technology are providing overwhelming amounts of easily accessible information that is inexpensive or free. Much of this information is being ostensibly identified by news gatherers and their disseminators as news, together with the implicit assumption of its truth. Thus, professional news gatherers (journalists) and their institutional news disseminators (news media) will now have even greater importance and value than in the past (1) when news gathering and dissemination processes were far more limited by time and space; (2) when these processes required far greater economic and other resources, particularly in the dissemination of news through the traditional mass media of print, radio, and television; and (3) when citizens and marketplace consumers faced far greater—oftentimes prohibitive—economic costs as well as insurmountable logistical barriers to access information, unlike today when a plethora of news and other information sources are readily available at little or no cost to the consumer.

Today, we are figuratively drowning in a sea of free or inconsequentially inexpensive information, much of it ostensibly from "news media" that cannot be trusted because of these news media's opacity that can hide myriad influences that result in incomplete truth. Thus, we argue that citizens and marketplace consumers will need to rely on professional journalists and their news media that (1) can be trusted as a source for news and other information that these professional journalists have gathered and/or verified and that their news media have disseminated using transparent methods that have no hidden influences; (2) identify and grade this news objectively and transparently; and (3) interpret this news fairly through transparent reasoning and methodologies. For journalists and their news media, the outcome of this successful effort to provide truth through media transparency will be the trust of citizens and marketplace consumers, and their reward will be the increased economic and intrinsic value of their product, the news.

News Media Opacity Is an Ethical Issue: Transparency Is the Responsibility of Journalists

In Chapter 2, we had argued that newsworthiness, that is, the significance and interest of truthful information that journalists and their news media have conscientiously gathered and/or verified, must be the sole criterion that determines this information's identification and dissemination as news in the news media. When newsworthiness is not the sole criterion in disseminating information that is proffered as news, we argued that other influences must be clearly identified and readily transparent. We concluded that news media opacity that hides incomplete truths is unquestionably an ethical issue, specifically that hidden influences in gathering and disseminating what is identified as news constitute a professional ethical transgression. But a professional ethical issue for whom?

We argue that it ultimately is the responsibility of journalists and their news media to assure news media transparency that prevents hidden influences in gathering and disseminating the news; journalists and their news media are the primary agents who must assume ultimate responsibility and accountability for the quality and integrity of their product, the news. However, multiple secondary actors are also culpable in news media opacity that hides influences, each of whom we argue must recognize and accept their share of ethical responsibility and accountability to assure news media transparency. Although they may have a variety of titles worldwide, we identified specifically those whose professional positions include primary responsibility for attempting to place media releases in the news media and for promoting themselves as sources for news; we call them public relations practitioners, as was explained in Chapter 2. Also sharing responsibility for news media transparency, albeit as stakeholders and not as a professional community, are citizens and marketplace consumers, that is, the consumers of news who must be vigilant in understanding the value and importance of transparency in the news media and in appreciating the dangers of news media opacity. These stakeholders must be cognizant of and sensitive to the range of hidden influences that can create incomplete truths. Consumers of news reasonably should expect—indeed must demand—transparency before giving journalists and their news media their trust, and these consumers are capable of enforcing this demand in multiple ways, not the least of which is their economic support as consumers of truth from transparent media.

In Chapter 2, we argued that each professional community must define its own role within—and responsibility toward—society by defining its professional ethics within the moral parameters of its society as well as within the laws of that society's government. These ethics define a professional community's relationship with its society, for which the professional community has at least some latitude and discretion in determining its professional ethics within those moral and legal parameters. It also is important to emphasize that one professional community does not have the right to dictate the ethics of another professional community that practices within the moral parameters of a society as well as within the laws of that society's government. Neither is a professional community able to enforce its ethics upon those who might practice that community's profession, but who are not a part of this professional community—for example, those practicing journalism or public relations who have chosen not to be part of these professional communities or whose membership has been rejected by those communities.

Given all of this, it is important to underscore several of this book's contentions. Particularly with today's overwhelming surfeit of communication channels and media, this book restricts its data, arguments, and recommendations to news as it has been defined; to the community of professional journalists as they have been defined; to their news media, again as they have been defined as a societal institution; and to the professional community of public relations practitioners who attempt to place news and other information in these news media and who promote themselves as sources for news.

Let us once again review what this book considers to be a journalist and what it defines as journalism. Kruckeberg (1995, pp. 78–79) acknowledged the complexities of the concept of journalism and the role of the journalist when he observed that we can be no more precise than to argue that "'journalism' is what 'journalists' do". He noted that a journalist could be a public affairs reporter of government activity or an advice columnist, an ideological interpreter of news for a propagandistic medium owned or sanctioned by an authoritarian government or a reporter for a commercially "controlled" medium. Kruckeberg (1995) attempted to identify which media and messages should be considered to be part of news media when he excluded special interest periodicals and media that are controlled by public relations practitioners, marketing communicators, and the like:

> Helpful is the identification of a predominant *general* news orienta-
> tion of qualifying media as a uniform and consistent threshold crite-
> rion. Public affairs reportage about journalists' respective governments
> likewise is a strong definitional component of such journalism as it is
> practiced in the general news media. (p. 79)

It is important to note that this book concerns itself with a highly restricted and exclusive "professional community" of journalists, usually those who self-identify and are accepted by their peers as being part of this community and whose credentials usually include a prescribed education in journalism's professional body of knowledge as well as a mas-
tery of professionally accepted requisite skills and abilities; adherence to a generally agreed-upon code of professional ethics; and, in many countries, professional licensure, albeit in other countries only voluntary credentials that give professional journalists a greater likelihood of success in an mar-
ket-determined unregulated profession, for example, a university degree in journalism and pre-professional training and experience. An example is the United States, where professional journalism cannot be licensed because every citizen has a First Amendment right to practice as a citizen what journalists practice professionally for news media. These journalists, after hav-
ing learned their professional knowledge, skills, and abilities, gather news and other information that are disseminated through news media to a gen-
eral audience through channels of communication that include newspapers, radio, and television stations as well as, more recently, through a range of new media. These are important distinctions in this book's discussion in an era when:

- Each citizen and marketplace consumer can become a self-declared ipso facto practicing journalist, that is, is free to perform the role of a journalist, with few or no professional or educational credentials or barriers to entry; no adherence to or even knowledge of professionally agreed-upon journalistic ethics; and no professional validation—thus, we do not include in this community of professional journalists everyone who ostensibly practices journalism and declares himself or herself to be a journalist, whether as bloggers or as participatory journalists or as active participants in the social media;
- When the popular concept of journalism arguably has become depro-
fessionalized because those wishing to practice journalism at whatever level no longer need a printing press, a radio, or television station, or must overcome other economic or resource barriers to entry—we

define journalism, its practice, and the news media restrictively and exclusively as described earlier;

- When longstanding professional practices and ethical values may be unknown, unappreciated, or are considered to be passé among those who portend to be journalists, but who are free to perform in the role of journalists—we declare the presentation of truth as we have defined it as a core, indeed ultimate, ethical value of professional journalism practice;
- In which the concepts of news and news values have become fluid and amorphous and oftentimes ideological, if not propagandistic, with no generally adhered-to professionally recognized news values; and ...
- When the agenda-setting role of the traditional mass media is becoming increasingly eroded and reactive because of the influence of an immense amount of readily available information, with news agendas becoming increasingly determined by non-journalist users of the social media.

The Question of Indigenous Societies' Histories, Cultures, and Ideologies

Of course, professional occupations such as journalism and societal institutions such as the news media also remain heavily influenced by, and indeed are usually predicated upon, their indigenous societies' histories, cultures, and ideologies. When arguing for universal ethical norms related to transparency and truth, questions of ethical and cultural relativism as well as the commonly perceived need for cultural tolerance inevitably must be considered and addressed. Earlier, we had noted that professional ethics are shaped by two distinct forces: (1) the wider moral principles of a society and (2) the aims of the occupation (Olen, 1988). Nevertheless, we have stated our strong belief that the need for news media transparency is universal, that is, we have argued that this need for news media transparency should be the norm for all indigenous societies worldwide and should be applicable to all professional journalists and their news media throughout the world. We do this despite our data that suggest that news media transparency is not the norm globally, nor is news media opacity universally condemned; indeed, it is oftentimes tacitly accepted. In few places is media opacity illegal, and any existing laws may be poorly and erratically enforced or be given little priority.

Of course when advocating for universal ethical norms calling for news media transparency and the dissemination of truth, we must examine the complex question of whether media opacity should indeed be accepted— or at least tolerated—in some situations and environments in deference to and respect for an indigenous society's history, culture, and ideology; for example, should not those hidden influences that are cloaked by news media opacity be assumed, if not tolerated, in cultures that have had long traditions in which "hidden" influences are abstractly transparent, even if specific examples might be opaque? Apologists for news media bribery and other hidden influences oftentimes cite the need for cultural tolerance because of:

- Journalists' low pay in some countries, a utilitarian argument that a greater good may result—or at least a lesser evil may occur—when, for example, a public relations agency representing a wealthy client bribes financially needy journalists and their revenue-starved news media to present incomplete truths that are advantageous to the client, particularly if everyone in this society ostensibly rationalizes that "this is the way the system works", while …
- Others excuse the supposedly immature and unsophisticated understanding of the role and function of a free press among sources, journalists, and their news media as well as citizens and marketplace consumers in newly emerging democracies and other lesser-developed countries—implicitly suggesting the need for patience and forbearance, sometimes with the stated assumption that the practice might ultimately disappear as these democracies continue to evolve. (Such an argument patronizingly suggests that some indigenous societies and their professional communities are not yet ready for—or perhaps are not even morally capable of—higher levels of ethical conduct and that citizens and marketplace consumers are not sufficiently sophisticated to appreciate the need for media transparency.)
- Accusations might also be heard concerning a perceived Western hegemony by public relations agencies and their transnational clients who resist paying bribes to indigenous news media, suggesting that active or passive resistance to this inferred cultural imperialism patriotically preserves long-standing indigenous traditions that are to be respected and venerated.
- Apologists frequently cite a carte blanche need for respect of (or at least tolerance for) all indigenous societies' prevailing social/economic/political traditions as well as for specific cultures' historical antecedents—with a plea for "cultural sensitivity" replete with a demand for tolerance, if not total and unquestioned acceptance, of these well-entrenched practices, no matter how offensive or deleterious they may appear to those outside of that culture.

Invariably, these and other arguments will be heard when news media transparency is advocated as a global norm and, conversely, when news media opacity that hides influences is condemned. At one level, many would submit that such arguments are obviously and absurdly flawed, indeed barely worthy of consideration or debate. At other levels, however, plausible, if not convincing, arguments can be presented for at least cultural tolerance, if not the validity and complete acceptance of a cultural relativism that declares all ethical and cultural beliefs to be equally valid.

Indeed, myriad rationale such as these are routinely cited to reject news media transparency on a global level when it is framed as a professional ethical issue for journalists and their news media as well as for public relations practitioners within their indigenous societies. Books have been written, and will continue to be written, about ethical and cultural relativism and the need to respect—if not accept carte blanche—the equal ethical validity of all cultures when recommendations are made about news media transparency as a universal value that conflicts with these indigenous societies' histories, cultures, and ideologies.

We Reject Cultural Relativity and Tolerance Related to News Media Transparency

This book rejects these arguments categorically, and the authors call for a worldwide universal norm for news media transparency and for the elimination of news media opacity that can hide influences. While we applaud and largely subscribe to a general sensitivity and overall respect for all indigenous societies' cultures, as well as an appreciation for their histories and a full consideration of their ideologies, we dismiss and consider to be irrelevant any concerns about cultural relativism and tolerance in our recommendations for news media transparency and in our castigation of media opacity that can hide influences that allow incomplete truth.

The two authors of this book take pride in their cosmopolitan worldview. One author is from the United States, and the other is from the former Soviet Union. We have traveled and lived extensively throughout the world; maintained close professional and personal relationships with a wide range of people globally; and are highly knowledgeable and respectful of many indigenous societies' histories, cultures, and ideologies worldwide. Both authors take pride in our openness toward and receptiveness of alternative worldviews and values, not only because of our liberal education and terminal degrees in the social sciences, but because of our extensive global life experiences. Furthermore, we can state categorically that neither of us has ever experienced the environment of an indigenous society in which our own values and assumption had not been reasonably, thought-provokingly, and credibly challenged; at every locale we have visited, we have observed practices and traditions, predicated on each society's unique history, culture, and ideology, that we readily acknowledged to be superior to that of our own cultures. Thus, when declaring the need for media transparency, we will not accept accusations of xenophobia or misplaced chauvinism, nor of ignorance or lack of respect of the histories, cultures, and ideologies of other societies throughout the world.

That said, we argue that indigenous societies' histories, cultures, and ideologies are irrelevant considerations when the need for media transparency and the assurance of truth are framed as ethical issues. Rather, we adamantly declare that media transparency and truth are universal values that should be shared among the professional communities of journalists, their news media, and public relations practitioners; furthermore, we strongly advocate that citizens and marketplace consumers must demand that these values be an integral part within the moral parameters of their societies. To re-emphasize, we believe media transparency that prevents hidden influences to assure truth in gathering and disseminating news should be a core value, regardless of any indigenous society's history, culture, and predominant ideology. Myriad arguments can be made in defense of our contentions that extend beyond laborious discussions about the need to respect the ethical validity of other cultures. However, the most pertinent arguments revolve around how a twenty-first-century global society can exist and survive as a continually evolving modernity becomes globally pervasive? We answer this fundamental question in the affirmative: Is truth a prerequisite for twenty-first-century global society to be sustainable, and, thus, is it an "ultimate value" for the entire world's people? We argue that truth through news media transparency is a requisite for a sustainable twenty-first-century global society.

At one level, a universal norm appears not to be possible. Ample evidence exists of an evolving global professionalization of journalists and of public relations practitioners, that is, global communities of professionals who share ethical values, as well as news media that share ethical values worldwide. Global norms can occur when professionals from throughout the world communicate among themselves and act together and when it becomes increasingly obvious that journalists in one part of the world share more similarities and values than differences with their counterparts elsewhere throughout the world, regardless of their indigenous cultures, histories, and ideologies.

Indeed, Kruckeberg (1998) predicted that globalization would encourage the universalization of professional public relations practice. He contended that personal and culture-based ethics would tend to become subsumed by "professional" ethics and these ethics' corresponding "professional" ethical values; multicultural perspectives would tend to become subsumed by a global professionalism that would tend to result in a solidarity of ethical assumptions based on increasingly common professional beliefs and ideologies; "professional" ethics would tend to become universal regardless of their professional application, client, or societal environment; practitioners of this "professionalized" occupation would tend to seek universals throughout societies on which to base their "professional" ethical behavior; and, as the value of public relations becomes increasingly recognized and as practitioners increasingly become part of an organization's dominant coalition, the range of multicultural perspectives in public relations would correspondingly decrease. Undoubtedly, the same could be said for the professional practice of journalism.

A Consensus about News Media Transparency Will Not Be Possible

However, even though we believe that news media transparency must be an ethical mandate and should be framed primarily as an ethical issue, we fully recognize and appreciate that such media transparency will not be universally valued as such, at least in the foreseeable future. This is in large part because of the irreconcilable perspectives that we have described, for which realistically a global consensus will not be reached at least for some time. Simply, many journalists and their news media, public relations practitioners, and citizens and marketplace consumers will not yield in their defense of their indigenous societies' cultural, historical, and ideological traditions that tolerate, if not support, news media opacity that hides influences that present incomplete truths. Thus, multiple global perspectives will not yield to a proposed need for a universal ethic of media transparency based on ethical arguments.

Also, a more insidious reason precludes a resistance toward media transparency. News media opacity is highly profitable for some journalists and their news media, and it can be highly advantageous to complicit public relations practitioners who want to promote their clients; thus, this news media opacity is often accepted by citizens and marketplace consumers —frequently with quiet resignation—as being inevitable, because simply, "This is the way the system works".

Conclusion

Thus, the need for media transparency that we frame as an obvious, albeit complex, ethical mandate is unlikely to reach a global moral consensus, not only because of disparate ethical perspectives worldwide, but also because hidden influences, which are made possible through media opacity, are highly profitable and advantageous to some journalists, their news media, and public relations practitioners and often are either unknown or are tacitly accepted by citizens and marketplace consumers.

Rather, with considerable irony, the need for media transparency is more likely to become universally accepted as a norm, or at least to become more highly valued, by framing news media transparency through arguments that are predicated on the premise that truth resulting from media transparency has both economic and intrinsic value and can be marketed effectively through branding. We will do so in the final chapter of this book. However, in the following chapters, let us examine how media opacity that hides influences creates incomplete truth throughout much of the world.

References

Kruckeberg, D. (1998, Spring). Future reconciliation of multicultural perspectives in public relations ethics. *Public Relations Quarterly*, 43(1), 45–48.

Kruckeberg, D. (1995). International journalism ethics. In J. C. Merrill (Ed.), *Global journalism: survey of international journalism*, 3rd edition (pp. 77–87). New York: Longman.

Olen, J. (1988). *Ethics in journalism*. Englewood Cliffs, NJ: Prentice Hall.

5   The Global Study of Media Transparency[1]

- Purpose: This chapter discusses the results of the global study on media transparency that was conducted by the authors to advance the theory and practice of media relations and to refine the categorization of determinants of media opacity resulting from various influences on the media that minimize or diminish media transparency.
- Method: A global online survey of members of four global professional associations (two journalism associations and two associations of public relations practitioners) was conducted to determine the landscape and self-reported perceptions of the presence of media non-transparent practices around the world. This study was based on previous country-by-country specific investigations into media non-transparent practices in various geographical regions that was conducted by the authors for over a decade.
- Results: Based on the analysis of the results from a global survey of 403 public relations practitioners and journalists who were members of four international professional associations, this study identified two major categories of the non-transparent practices: (1) influences and (2) monetary and non-monetary compensations. Additionally, the results demonstrated that a higher frequency of the non-transparent practices across these two dimensions resulted in a lower level of perceived media credibility. Finally, the study also demonstrated that, despite the fact that the media bribery practices occur worldwide, the majority of professionals unanimously deny that these practices are professional, acceptable, and ethical.
- Recommendations: Empirical tests demonstrated that determinants of media non-transparency and credibility are negatively correlated, indicating that the higher frequency of the non-transparent practices results in a lower level of the perceived media credibility.

1 The authors would like to acknowledge Anna Klyueva, University of Houston–Clear Lake, as the third author of this chapter.

- Conclusions: The importance of the new categorization that provides a more comprehensive understanding of media opacity and study implications for media relations practice and future research is discussed.

Media transparency exists when a public relations practitioner presents an information subsidy to a news medium, which may or may not disseminate this media release based solely on its newsworthiness, not because of monetary or other hidden influences (Kruckeberg, 1995). Throughout the world, news media and their representatives constantly experience pressures from public relations practitioners as well as from advertisers, information sources, publishers, and other influential groups (Kruckeberg & Tsetsura, 2003).

Transparency of news media reflects how information subsidies (Gandy, 1982) are being produced, delivered, and used by media professionals. Understanding media transparency is fundamental to understanding the relationship between journalists and public relations practitioners. Journalism and public relations professional organizations throughout the world consider media transparency as a means to diminish unethical and illegal practices in the relationships between public relations practitioners and the media (IPRA, 2004).

Media transparency is a normative concept that is rooted in ethical theory, lying at the cross-section of different ethical perspectives. Media transparency has deontological roots, because its inherent attribute is the duty to tell the truth (Denise, 1999). However, transparency also considers the moral character of the truth-teller and the motivation behind his or her truth-telling. Thus, transparency is defined differently by different disciplines as well as by individual scholars. Plaisance (2007) draws from a range of theorists when he proposes to treat transparent behavior "as conduct that presumes openness in communication and serves a reasonable expectation of forthright exchange when parties have a legitimate stake in the possible outcomes or effects of the communicative act" (p. 188).

Tsetsura and Kruckeberg (2009) proposed that news media transparency can be achieved when several conditions are met. First, many competing sources of information should be used, that is, there cannot be a single source of truth for a journalist. For news media to be transparent and for journalists to exhibit transparent behavior, multiple competing sources of truth must used. Second, the method of information delivery should be known. In other words, journalists and news media must be transparent about the channels through which these truths were available to journalists. Third, the source of funding for media production should be evident and publicly available (Tsetsura & Kruckeberg, 2009). This means that, for a journalist (and the journalist's medium) to be transparent, any ulterior motives or interests of the journalist that might exist in the truth-telling must also be revealed.

It is clear that truth is an inherent attribute of transparency; however, transparency and truth are not the same. The concept of truth helps to understand why transparency is important for media and journalism. According to Kant, truth is grounded in people's ability to be rational and to exercise free will (Denise, 1999). Therefore, deception or lack of transparency dehumanizes media's audiences by limiting their ability to exercise free will and to shape informed opinions and judgments about issues. Yet, transparency is not an absolutist concept. Plaisance (2007) argues that transparency does nothing to reduce a deception that did not exist.

Therefore, this book investigates what deceptive practices undermine media transparency throughout the world. Because media transparency is a normative concept, it is difficult to measure it directly. One way to assess media transparency is to examine its antithesis—media non-transparency, that is, media opacity. The terms media non-transparency and media opacity are commonly used to study non-transparent media practices, such as hidden payments for news coverage and other indirect influences on the news media (Kruckeberg & Tsetsura, 2003; Tsetsura, 2005b; Tsetsura & Grynko, 2009). In Russia, this phenomenon was initially known as *zakazukha*, a Russian slang word for paid publicity (Holmes, 2001). Different studies have employed different descriptions of this phenomenon: cash for news coverage (Kruckeberg & Tsetsura, 2003), media bribery (Tsetsura, 2005b), media non-transparency (Tsetsura & Grynko, 2009), and media opacity (Tsetsura & Kruckeberg, 2009). This book uses the terms media non-transparency and media opacity interchangeably.

Previous studies of media transparency have been conducted throughout the world (Kruckeberg & Tsetsura, 2003; Kruckeberg, Tsetsura, & Ovaitt, 2005). In addition, four empirical country-specific studies have examined practices in China (Tsetsura, 2015), Poland (Tsetsura, 2005b), Russia (Klyueva, 2008; Tsetsura, 2005a), and Ukraine (Tsetsura & Grynko, 2009). While insights on media transparency from these countries are important, an examination is needed to determine whether non-transparent practices exist globally to help determine the underlying global structure of these practices. It is particularly important to examine news media opacity as a major factor that defines and influences the media relations of public relations practitioners (Tsetsura & Kruckeberg, 2009). This chapter provides an overview and summarizes research about theories of information subsidies that are relevant to news media transparency and summarizes research on the topic.

Information Subsidy

The concept of the information subsidy (Gandy, 1982) helps to frame the complex relationship between journalists and public relations practitioners.

Gandy defined an information subsidy as information that is generated by a public relations practitioner to publicize his or her organization, its products, or a specific point of view. He argued that the use of an information subsidy is an effort to decrease the cost of information for news media representatives to enhance consumption of this information. The use of information subsidies has economic implications for both news media and public relations practitioners, the latter who invest resources to produce information subsidies that media organizations basically receive for free (Zoch & Molleda, 2006). Originally, an information subsidy was conceptualized as "editorial content that public relations practitioners provide free of charge to media" (Grunig & Hunt, 1984, p. 46).

According to Gandy (1982), subsidized information is usually less credible to the consumer of this information because of the relationship between perceived credibility and the source's interest in publicizing this information. Therefore, public relations practitioners are often interested in delivering an "undercover subsidy", in which the source's interests are disguised. Gandy criticized information subsidies for their direct and indirect influence on media content; he argued that information subsidies corrupt the process of news gathering because larger organizations have more resources to create these information subsidies and to provide background information for news stories. According to Gandy, smaller organizations that lack resources cannot compete with larger organizations. As a result, their points of view would not appear in the news as often.

However, other scholars (Taylor, 2000; Taylor & Doerfel, 2003) argue that information subsidies have enormous potential to help place important social issues on the public agenda. These information subsidies allow for establishing positive, mutually beneficial relationships between journalists and public relations practitioners and demonstrate how public relations practitioners and journalists need to interact to create news content. Taylor (2009) argued that news media organizations need information and public relations practitioners need a channel of communication to reach their targeted audiences. She said that this is particularly true in those parts of the world where media relations is a relatively new phenomenon.

Yet, Taylor (2009) recognized that information subsidies taken to an extreme may damage the credibility of the news media, as well as the value of the news stories that are generated by public relations practitioners. In pursuit of publicity, news sources may attempt to exert influence over media or to bribe media representatives when subsidizing information (Kruckeberg & Tsetsura, 2003). On the other hand, media commercialization and concentration force some news media to adopt more and more market principles (Herman & Chomsky, 1988). In pursuit of advertising revenue, some news media are ready to compromise their professional integrity, sometimes allowing their advertising departments to influence the decisions of editors (Tsetsura, 2005b).

Therefore, media transparency is defined as public relations practitioners' presentation of information subsidies to news media, which may or may not disseminate these media releases based solely on their newsworthiness, but not because of monetary or other hidden influences (Kruckeberg, 1995). When a news medium disseminates information to consumers because of hidden monetary or non-monetary compensations, the transparency of the news medium is compromised as well as that news medium's credibility. In addition, the mutually beneficial relationship between journalists and public relations practitioners is also weakened. Research on media transparency is particularly concerned with opaque media practices in which subsidized information is disseminated by news media in exchange for direct or indirect payments. The next section of this chapter provides an overview of research on media transparency.

Global Media Transparency Research

Early research on media transparency was conducted by Kruckeberg and Tsetsura in 2003 when they developed and published the first global index that ranked 66 of the world's nation-states for the likelihood that journalists working for the top ten daily newspapers in each of these countries would seek or accept cash payments for news coverage from government officials, businesses, or other news sources. Kruckeberg and Tsetsura (2003) used primary data of an expert survey among representatives of global professional associations in journalism (International Press Institute, International Federation of Journalists) and public relations (International Public Relations Association) to study eight determinants that might affect media bribery in these countries: (1) long-time tradition of self-determination by citizens, (2) comprehensive corruption laws with effective enforcement, (3) accountability of government to citizens at all levels, (4) high adult literacy, (5) high liberal and professional education of practicing journalists, (6) well-established, publicized, and enforceable journalism codes of professional ethics, (7) free press, free speech, and free flow of information, and (8) high media competition (multiple and competing media). Then, the authors used the secondary data from nine worldwide databases to assign one of 33 rankings to 66 countries according to the likelihood of problems with media transparency, that is, likely media bribery. Although variables the authors used to rank countries are comprehensive, the index did not directly measure the phenomenon of cash for coverage according to perceptions of practitioners. However, the secondary data collected provided a good benchmark, especially for the first published media transparency research.

Finland ranked first on the index, meaning there is very little likelihood that cash-for-coverage exists. The United States ranked fifth out of 33 ranks of 66 countries in the index. According to the results of this study, media bribery was most likely to occur in China, Saudi Arabia, Vietnam, Bangladesh, and Pakistan. By contrast, countries with the best ratings for the likelihood of avoiding these practices were Finland (first place) and Denmark, New Zealand, and Switzerland (tied for second place). Germany, Iceland, and the United Kingdom tied for third place, followed by Norway (fourth place). Austria, Canada, the Netherlands, Sweden, Belgium, and the United States had the fifth best ratings (Kruckeberg & Tsetsura, 2003).

This research was performed as part of a campaign for media transparency that was initiated by the Institute for Public Relations and the International Public Relations Association (IPRA, 2004). This campaign was designed to attract public attention and to fight media non-transparency throughout the world. In 2004, six global organizations announced their support for a set of principles designed to foster greater transparency in the dealings between public relations practitioners and the news media and to end bribery for media coverage throughout the world (Kruckeberg, Tsetsura, & Ovaitt, 2005). These organizations were the International Press Institute, International Federation of Journalists, Transparency International, the Global Alliance for Public Relations and Communications Management, the Institute for Public Relations, and the International Public Relations Association (IPRA, 2004).

This research project generated a lot of attention from media professionals throughout the world. In 2005, a follow-up investigation of media practices (Tsetsura, 2005b) was conducted in Poland to learn what forms of news media non-transparency existed. Tsetsura (2005b) found that cash for news coverage is just part of the problem. Her research showed that the phenomenon of media non-transparency has at least two dimensions: (1) direct and indirect payments and influences on the media, and (2) different types of media, such as local and regional and national media. Direct payments were defined as cash or other monetary payments for news coverage (Kruckeberg & Tsetsura, 2003). Indirect payments and influences were defined "as any type of non-monetary reward to a journalist, editor, or media outlet or the existence of a media policy which dictates, encourages indirect payments or influences the financial success and independence of the media outlet or its employees" (Tsetsura, 2005b, p. 15).

Indirect payments are more complicated because they can take any imaginable form. As a result of this study, Tsetsura (2005b) developed the following classification of the types of indirect payments and influences: (1) publication or production of materials in exchange for paid advertising, (2) written media rules of conduct that allow the receipt of samples, free gifts, or attractively discounted items from third parties to media representatives, (3) conflict of interest when a journalist is employed by both a news medium and a company, institution, government, or public relations agency, (4) pressure from the advertising departments of news media on editors regarding which news from which sources to cover, and (5) financial and psychological pressure from news sources, companies, and public relations agencies on the news media to disseminate information that had come from these sources.

Previous research in Poland demonstrated that media professionals were more concerned with indirect cases of media non-transparency, specifically with publishing publicity materials in exchange for advertising in the same medium and putting financial pressure on news media to present information coming from news sources, such as companies and public relations agencies (Tsetsura, 2005b). A similar study was conducted in Ukraine (Tsetsura & Grynko, 2009). Tsetsura and Grynko found that media non-transparency has three different levels of relationships between journalists and public relations practitioners: interpersonal, intra-organizational, and inter-organizational. At the interpersonal level, non-transparent media practices happen privately between individual journalists and public relations practitioners. At the intra-organizational level, non-transparent media practices occur when advertising sales departments and news media administration can influence decisions of editors regarding what information from which sources will be disseminated to the news media's consumers. Finally, at the inter-organizational level, non-transparent media practices happen when news media sign formal contracts with other organizations and those contracts dictate what information should be covered by the news media. Confirming previous studies of media non-transparent practices, Klyueva (2008) discovered that both direct and indirect payments and influences are present in the Russian media. Using the example of local and regional media in the Urals District of Russia, Klyueva also demonstrated that media non-transparent practices can be formalized in a written policy that outlines the terms of acceptance of these practices. Another study showed that, in China, media non-transparency most often happens in the local and regional media (Tsetsura & Grynko, 2009).

Previous research on media transparency revealed several patterns that are common across borders and cultures. First, studies confirmed that problems with media transparency exist almost everywhere, although with a variation in degree of transparency. Second, previous studies on media transparency developed a categorization of non-transparent media practices. Particularly, studies in Russia (Klyueva, 2008; Tsetsura, 2005a), Poland (Tsetsura, 2005b), China (Tsetsura, 2015), and Ukraine (Tsetsura & Grynko, 2009) confirmed that different types of direct and indirect payments and influences exist in different countries. However, no previous research had tested this categorization systematically around the world. Therefore, it is necessary to examine whether the classification of non-transparent practices as direct and indirect payments and influences is valid and is present globally. It is also important to examine whether the different types of non-transparent media practices affect the perceived credibility of the news media as theories of information subsidies suggest. Thus, this study had two goals: first, to examine the underlying dimensions of non-transparent practices in the news media; and, second, to examine whether the different types of non-transparent practices affect media credibility. Therefore, the following research questions were formulated for this global study:

RQ1: What is the underlying dimension structure of the non-transparent media practices around the world?

RQ2: Is there a relationship between the perceived frequency of the non-transparent media practices and the perceived credibility of the media around the world?

RQ3: How do members of global professional communities perceive these practices?

Method

The data for this study were collected through an online survey in fall 2007. The population included individual members of three major professional journalism and public relations associations: the International Federation of Journalists (N = 134), International Public Relations Association (N = 1,140), and International Press Institute (N = 1,000). In addition, representatives of all 66 association members of the Global Alliance were invited to participate in the study (the Global Alliance does not have individual memberships). Members of all associations were invited to participate in the study. A four-step distribution process was used, and letters of invitation were sent to all potential participants once a week during a four-week period. This follow-up correspondence was conducted in accordance with Dilman's (1978) recommendations, who argued that this method allows the researcher to maximize the response rate. The researchers obtained 403 usable responses (journalists n = 93; public relations practitioners n = 310), yielding an overall response rate of 17.2 percent (8.2 percent for journalists and 25.7 percent for public relations practitioners).

Instrument

This study utilized a survey that had been previously developed for other studies of media non-transparency in several countries. The survey consisted of multi-layered questions that were constructed to explore the phenomenon across two dimensions: (1) different types of media and (2) different types of direct and indirect payments and influences. For this study, only nine survey items were analyzed. The first eight items represented different types of direct and indirect payments and influences as described by Tsetsura (2005b) and as outlined in Table 5.1. These survey items represented composite variables, which included measures for six types of media: (1) national daily newspaper, (2) national TV programming, (3) national radio programming, (4) local and regional daily newspaper, (5) local and regional TV programming, and (6) local and regional radio programming. In these survey questions, respondents were asked to record their perceived levels of frequency of occurrence of non-transparent media practices along a five-point semantic differential scale, from 1 (*never*) to 5 (*always*). For example, respondents had to rate how frequently the following practice takes place in each of the six media types: "News sources put financial pressure on the media (such as withholding advertising, government subsidies, etc.) to influence media news judgment". Statement responses were coded so that the higher value indicated support of the concept, meaning that the media practices were less transparent. Three questions of the survey were reverse coded for logic in data analysis (see Table 5.1). The internal reliability of each composite variable was satisfactory and ranged from $\alpha = .901$ to $\alpha = .970$.

The perceived credibility of the media was also measured through a five-point semantic differential scale, from 1 (*low*) to 5 (*high*). The respondents were asked to rate the perceived credibility of the media in their respective countries. This survey item also represented a composite variable constructed out of credibility measures of the outlined above six media types. The internal reliability of this scale was also satisfactory ($\alpha = .950$).

Table 5.1 Types of direct and indirect payments and influences (initially theorized by Tsetsura, 2005b, and used in this study)

		n	M	SD
V3*	Material which appears in print or on air as a result of direct payment is clearly identified as advertising or paid-for promotion and is not disguised as editorial	336	2.53	.832
V5*	When a journalist or an editor has benefited from the provision of a product or service, such as a hotel stay or keeping the equipment tested, this is identified alongside the resulting report	330	3.44	1.096

(continued)

Table 5.1 Types of direct and indirect payments and influences (initially theorized by Tsetsura, 2005b and used in this study) (*continued*)

		n	*M*	*SD*
V6*	News media have a written policy covering the receipt of samples, free gifts or discounted materials from news sources	304	3.12	1.055
V8	A news release that is not newsworthy appears in a publication in exchange for paid advertising placed in the same publication	307	2.92	.899
V9	An advertisement is produced to look like a regular article or program and there is nothing that clearly informs the reader that the message has been paid for	304	2.66	.852
V11	A journalist who has a conflict of interest is also employed as a news source by a company/institution/government or agency, and this is not clearly disclosed in his or her news report	286	2.72	.983
V12	An advertising sales department of a media outlet influences the decisions of editors in terms of which news from which sources gets covered	293	2.89	.858
V14	News sources put financial pressure on the media (such as withholding advertising, government subsidies, etc.) to influence media news judgment	294	2.99	.904

Note: *indicates reverse coding

Data Analysis

To answer Research Question 1, a principal components analysis (PCA) was performed on eight survey items that represented different types of initially theorized direct and indirect payments and influences. PCA was used because it explores overall variability of the data and helps to generate a minimum number of components that account for the maximum number of variance in the data (Tabachnik & Fidell, 2007). The goal of PCA is to find a structure that explains maximum variance with the smallest number of factors. Prior to performing PCA, the suitability of the data for factor analysis was assessed. Examination of the correlation matrix revealed the presence of many coefficients of .3 and above. Overall factorability of the data was good (MSA = .867 and x^2 [df = 28] = 667.356, $p < .001$), and univariate MSA values were also acceptable (that is, all items were greater than .60).

The only reason for PCA limitation would be weak loadings, less than .4. All loadings in this study were bigger than .55.

To answer Research Question 2, which asked whether there was a relationship between the perceived frequency of the non-transparent media practices and the perceived credibility of these media, a correlation analysis was performed and a Pearson product-moment correlation coefficient was calculated. In addition, preliminary analyses were performed to ensure that there was no violation of the assumption of normality, linearity, and homoscedasticity. The results of the analyses are reported in the next section.

Results

The first research question asked whether there was an underlying structure of the global dimensions of media non-transparency. Principal components analysis revealed the presence of two components with eigenvalues exceeding 1, explaining 41 percent of the variance for the first component and 22.7 percent of the variance for the second component. The two-component solution was further supported by Cattell's (1966) scree test and 95th percentile parallel analysis (Horn, 1965; O'Connor, 2000). The final two-component solution explained a total of 63.7 percent of the variance. To aid in the interpretation of these two components, varimax (orthogonal) rotation was performed. The rotation solution revealed the presence of simple structure (Thurstone, 1947), with no loadings less than .55 on one component (see Table 5.2).

Table 5.2 Summary of results of principal components analysis

Item	# of items	Factor loadings	Communalities
Influences (α = .854)	5		
V8. A news release that is not newsworthy appears in a publication in exchange for paid advertising placed in the same publication		.838	.722
V9. An advertisement is produced to look like a regular article or program and there is nothing that clearly informs the reader that the message has been paid for		.773	.659

(continued)

Table 5.2 Summary of results of principal components analysis (*continued*)

Item	# of items	Factor loadings	Communalities
V11. A journalist who has a conflict of interest is also employed as a news source by a company/institution/ government or agency, and this is not clearly disclosed in his or her news report		.763	.590
V12. An advertising sales department of a media outlet influences the decisions of editors in terms of which news from which sources gets covered		.762	.686
V14. News sources put financial pressure on the media (such as withholding advertising, government subsidies, etc.) to influence media news judgment		.749	.600
Monetary and non-monetary compensations (α = .592)	3		
V3. Material which appears in print or on air as a result of direct payment is *not* clearly identified as advertising or paid-for promotion and *is* disguised as editorial		.737	.624
V5. When a journalist or an editor has benefited from the provision of a product or service, such as a hotel stay or keeping the equipment tested, this is *not* identified alongside the resulting report		.855	.731
V6. News media have a written policy covering the receipt of samples, free gifts or discounted materials from news sources		.553	.486

Note: The total proportion of variance explained is 63.7%.

The first component (α = .854) of the final two-component solution included the following items: (1) a news release that is not newsworthy appears in a publication in exchange for paid advertising placed in the same publication (V8); (2) an advertisement is produced to look like a regular article or program, and there is nothing that clearly informs the reader that the message has been paid for (V9); (3) a journalist who has a conflict of interest is also employed as a news source by a company/institution/government or agency, and this is not clearly disclosed in his or her news report (V11); (4) an advertising sales department of a news medium influences decisions of the editors in terms of which news from which sources gets covered (V12); and (5) news sources put financial pressure on the media (such as withholding advertising, government subsidies, etc.) to influence media news judgment (V14). The second component (α = .592) included the following items: (1) material that appears in print or on air as a result of direct payment is clearly identified as advertising or paid-for promotion and is not disguised as editorial (V3); (2) when a journalist or an editor has benefited from the provision of a product or service, such as a hotel stay or keeping the equipment that was tested, this is identified alongside the resulting report (V5); and (3) news media have a written policy covering the receipt of samples, free gifts, or discounted materials from news sources (V6).

After close examination of the items in each component, the first component was labelled "influences" because all items represented different types of influence on media content without any direct payments. The second component was labelled "monetary and non-monetary compensations" because all items represented different types of material compensations for media coverage from news sources. Overall, the discovered structure of the non-transparent media practices neither confirmed nor rejected the existing categorization. However, extracted components did not have a clear division between direct and indirect payments and influences.

Research Question 2 asked whether a relationship exists between the perceived frequency of non-transparent media practices and the perceived level of media credibility. A strong negative correlation was found between the two dimensions of media non-transparency and the perceived level of media credibility: influences and monetary and non-monetary compensations. Particularly, results indicated that the dimension "influences" explained about 21 percent of the variance in the respondents' scores on the perceived media credibility ($r = -.460, n = 218, p < .001$). The dimension "monetary and non-monetary compensations" also had a significant correlation with perceived media credibility and explained about 18 percent of the variance ($r = -.432, n = 226, p < .001$). These findings indicated that a higher frequency of the non-transparent practices across two dimensions resulted in a lower level of the perceived media credibility.

Research Question 3 asked how members of global professional communities perceive these practices. The results showed that the members indicated different forms of media bribery practices occur on a regular basis in their countries, according to their perceptiosn of practices (see Figure 5.1). However, when they were asked how they personally perceive these practices, the vast majority of respondents indicated that they perceive these practices as unaceptable (see Figure 5.2).

Discussion

The idea behind the concept of media transparency is that it ought to limit deception and misinformation. According to Plaisance (2007), even when

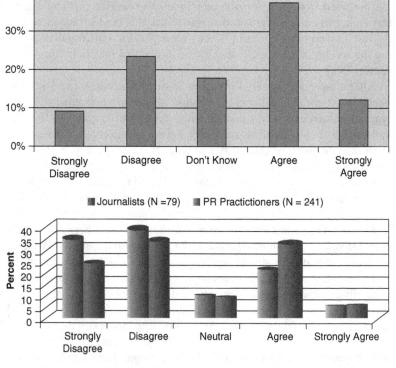

Figure 5.1 It is considered OK to accept payments by national media in my country? (N = 320)

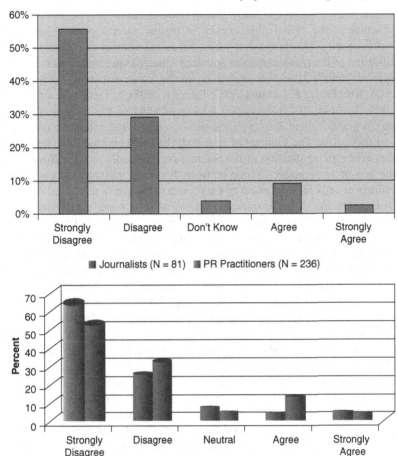

Figure 5.2 Do you *personally* agree this practice is acceptable? (N = 317; M = 1.74; SD = 1.06)

transparency is not always a sufficient condition for the ethical behavior of a journalist, the absence of transparency "is a prerequisite for deception, which presents serious challenges for anyone who values ethical behaviour" (p. 193). As Plaisance argued, upholding transparency is not an absolute decision-making mechanism for media and for journalism. However, by being transparent, journalists simply demonstrate that they are ethical from the start. This study contributes to further discussions of media transparency and the importance of media transparency in mass communication and media studies.

The main goal of this study was to uncover the underlying dimension structure of the global phenomenon of media non-transparency, that is, media opacity. This is the first study that tested whether the current classification of the non-transparent practices is indeed appropriate and can be applied globally. Previous studies on media non-transparency (Klyueva, 2008; Kruckeberg & Tsetsura, 2003; Tsetsura, 2005a, b; Tsetsura & Grynko, 2009; Tsetsura, 2015) developed a categorization of the non-transparent media practices that distinguished between direct and indirect payments and influences. The findings of this study neither confirmed nor rejected this existing classification of the determinants of media opacity. However, the lack of an apparent division between direct and indirect payments and influences calls for refinement of the present categorization.

Examination of the extracted components in this study indicated that the prior categorization was not exhaustive and that determinants of non-transparent practices could fall under both direct and indirect payments and influences. For example, a practice such as publication of non-newsworthy information in exchange for paid advertising placed in the same media can be described as both direct and indirect payment and influence. To avoid such confusion in future studies, this study offers a refined classification of the non-transparent media practices: (1) influences and (2) monetary and non-monetary compensations.

Influences are defined as deliberate actions of news sources that produce effects on the actions, behaviors, opinions, etc., of the media. Influences mostly happen at the intra-organizational level (when the hierarchical structure of the media may exert influence on media content) and the inter-organizational level (when different institutions exert influence on the media that is expressed in media content) (Tsetsura & Grynko, 2009). Five major types of influences were identified as a result of this study: (1) publication or production of materials in exchange for paid advertising; (2) a disguise of an advertisement as a regular article; (3) conflict of interests when a journalist is employed by the media and a company, institution, government, or public relations agency; (4) pressure from the advertising departments of media on editors regarding which news from which sources to cover; and (5) financial pressure from news sources, companies, and public relations agencies on the media to present information that comes from them.

Compensations are defined as payments given or received as an equivalent for the offered services and products. Compensations usually happen at the interpersonal level, when news sources try to exert influence on a particular journalist to receive favorable publicity (Tsetsura & Grynko, 2009), but they may also be institutionalized within an organization in the form of policy (Klyueva, 2008). Two major types of compensations can be identified based on the results of previous studies: (1) monetary compensations that can be produced in any form of payments, and (2) non-monetary compensations, when a media representative benefits from the provision of a product or service, such as a hotel stay or equipment (Tsetsura, 2005b, Tsetsura, 2015).

The results of this study also demonstrated that the more media non-transparent practices are present, according to the media and public relations professionals, the less credible the media are perceived to be in that country. This is an important finding that supports our claim about the diminishing trust in the media as a result of increasing media bribery. In many countries throughout the world, the gradual change toward new trends in the media that blend news pages, editorial pages, and/or promotional materials of advertising, of a paid nature, is alarming. Some call it a native advertising, others sponsored content or brand journalism. However, the difference between what is paid and what is not is increasingly smudged, which presents a great opening for media opacity.

Finally, the results have demonstrated that the vast majority of respondents, media, and public relations practitioners who are members of major global professional associations in both fields, journalism and public relations, reported that, although they believe these media bribery practices are common in their countries, this practice is unacceptable. That means that there is a clear gap between knowing and doing in terms of media bribery: one on hand, many claim this is a common practice; on the other hand, many argue this is an unacceptable practice.

So why does this gap exist? We argue that this practice is perceived as unacceptable because practitioners worldwide recognize the challenges of diminishing trust in societies, increasingly the call for transparency. Media transparency has become one of the most common professional expectations of public relations practices in the twenty-first century. Multiple studies have shown that practitioners are concerned about media opacity and often label it problematic, if not unethical (Tsetsura & Aziz, 2015; Tsetsura & Grynko, 2009; Klyueva & Tsetsura, 2010, 2011; Tsetsura, 2015; Tsetsura & Luoma-aho, 2010; Nguyen & Tsetsura, 2015). Yet, media non-transparency practices are widespread in many countries, and often practitioners face a challenging decision-making process: to give in to media bribery to receive media coverage. The problem is that every time this transaction occurs—and it is not clearly marked or labeled in the final media product—the credibility of the media outlet, and the credibility of the company (and a PR practitioner), is diminished. Nonetheless, media opacity practices continue to be present in many parts of the world.

How do we change this practice? The best way to address the problematics of media opacity is to create opportunities for professionals in their own professional communities throughout the world to openly and actively discuss media opacity and the consequences of this practice. The early research in media bribery in Poland allowed Polish professionals to do just that: practitioners and journalists got together and spent a considerable amount of time discussing media bribery and developing ethical codes of standards for both journalists and public relations practitioners, as a result of the Polish media bribery study by (Tsetsura, 2005b). Whether these conversations lead to actions, such as the development of codes of conduct, guidelines to resist media opacity, or professional agreements to recognize this practice as non-ethical, discussions and debates must take place among practitioners, scholars, and all professionals in both fields, journalism and public relations, if we are to move forward in re-establishing trust in societies.

Conclusion and Recommendations for Future Studies

This global study advanced the theory and practice of media relations by refining the categorization of determinants of media opacity, a result of various influences on the media that minimize or diminish media transparency. Based on an analysis of the results from a global survey of 403 public relations practitioners and journalists, who were members of four international professional associations, this study proposed two major categories of non-transparent practices: (1) influences and (2) monetary and non-monetary compensations. The results of this study confirmed that both influences and monetary and non-monetary compensations may damage credibility of the media. The higher frequency of these non-transparent practices in the media results in a lower level of media credibility as perceived by media professionals.

The refined classification of the determinants of media opacity has allowed testing media opacity effects on media credibility. As predicted by Gandy (1982) and Taylor (2009), this study has demonstrated that, when the exchange of information subsidies is produced with any monetary or non-monetary compensation or by influencing media, the transparency of the news media is usually compromised and so is media credibility. Media professionals and members of the global professional associations who reported the presence of the non-transparent practices (influences and monetary and non-monetary compensations) in the media of their countries also acknowledged that these practices affect news media credibility. This finding calls for further, more detailed examination of the reasons why media professionals in different countries contribute to media opacity, even when they realize that media opacity affects the credibility of the news media.

Overall, the results of this study have propelled our understanding of the underlying structure of non-transparent media practices and have refined the classification of the determinants of media non-transparency, that is, media opacity. This research also has demonstrated the relationship between the determinants of media opacity and media credibility. Additional research is needed to further explore the effect of media opacity on the perceptions of news media credibility and whether this perception is different between journalists and public relations practitioners. Future studies should also test the refined categorization of the determinants of media opacity with a different sample of global media professionals to determine whether this structure is sustainable within different sample groups.

The next chapter discusses several ways to stimulate conversations and debates among professional communities to address media opacity and to develop guidelines for practitioners in different regions—and worldwide.

References

Cattell, R. B. (1966). The scree test for number of factors. *Multivariate Behavioral Research, 1*, 245–276.

Denise, T. C. (1999). *Great traditions in ethics*. New York: Peter Lang.

Dilman, D. (1978). *The total design method*. New York: John Wiley & Sons.

Gandy, O. H., Jr. (1982). *Beyond agenda setting: Information subsidies and public policy*. Norwood, NJ: Ablex.

Grunig, J. E., & Hunt, T. (1984). *Managing public relations*. New York: Holt, Rinehart & Winston.

Herman, E., & Chomsky, N. (1988). *Manufacturing consent*. New York: Pantheon Books.

Holmes, P. (2001, March 5). Russian PR firm exposes media corruption. *The Holmes Report, 1*(9). Retrieved from www.holmesreport.com/story.cfm?edit_id=156&typeid=1.

Horn, J. L. (1965). A rationale and test for a number of factors in factor analysis. *Psychometrika, 30*, 179–185.

IPRA, International Public Relations Association (2004). *Development of the campaign for media transparency*. Retrieved from www.ipra.org/detail.asp?articleid=147.

Klyueva, A. (2008). *An exploratory study of media transparency in the Urals Federal District of Russia*. Unpublished master's thesis, University of Oklahoma, Norman, OK.

Klyueva, A., & Tsetsura, K. (2011). News from the Urals with love and payment: The first look at non-transparent media practices in the Urals Federal District of Russia. *Russian Journal of Communication, 4*(1/2), 72–93.

Klyueva, A., & Tsetsura, K. (2010). Media non-transparency research: A case of Romania. *Public Relations Journal, 4*(4). Retrieved from www.prsa.org/Intelligence/PRJournal/Documents/2010FallKlyuevaTsetsura.pdf.

Kruckeberg, D. (1995). International journalism ethics. In J. C. Merrill (Ed.), *Global journalism: Survey of international communication* (pp. 77–87). White Plains, NY: Longman.

Kruckeberg, D., & Tsetsura, K. (2003). International index of bribery for news coverage. *Institute for Public Relations Report: International Research*. Retrieved from www.instituteforpr.org/bribery-news-coverage-2003/.

Kruckeberg, D., Tsetsura, K., & Ovaitt, F. (2005). International index of media bribery. In *The Global Corruption Report 2005: Transparency International* (pp. 258–261). London: Pluto Press.

Nguyen, T. T., & Tsetsura, K. (2015, May). *Gift in our life: How gift-giving culture affects media relations in Vietnam*. Competitively selected paper presented at the 2015 annual ICA conference, San Juan, Puerto Rico.

O'Connor, B. P. (2000). Using parallel analysis and Velicer's MAP test. *Behavior Research Methods, Instruments, & Computers, 32*, 396–402.

Plaisance, P. (2007). Transparency: An assessment of Kantian roots of a key element in media ethics practice. *Journal of Mass Media Ethics, 22*, 208–214.

Tabachnik, B. G., & Fidell, L. S. (2007). *Using multivariate statistics* (5th ed.). Boston: Pearson.

Taylor, M. (2009). Protocol journalism as a framework for understanding public relations-media relationships in Kosovo. *Public Relations Review, 35*, 23–30.

Taylor, M. (2000). Media relations in Bosnia: A role for public relations in building civil society. *Public Relations Review, 26*, 1–14.

Taylor, M., & Doerfel, M. L. (2003). Building inter-organizational relationships that build nations. *Human Communication Research, 29*, 153–181.

Thurstone, L. L. (1947). *Multiple factor analysis*. Chicago: University of Chicago Press.

Tsetsura, K. (2015). Guanxi, gift-giving, or bribery? Ethical considerations of paid news in China. *Public Relations Journal, 9*(2). Retrieved from www.prsa.org/Intelligence/PRJournal/Documents/2015v09n02Tsetsura.pdf.

Tsetsura, K. (2005a). The exploratory study of media transparency and cash for news coverage practice in Russia: Evidence from Moscow PR agencies. *Proceedings of the 8th International Interdisciplinary Public Relations Research Conference*, Miami, FL: University of Miami.

Tsetsura, K. (2005b). Bribery for news coverage: Research in Poland (peer-reviewed research article). *Institute for Public Relations Online: International Research*. Retrieved from www.instituteforpr.com/international.phtml.

Tsetsura, K., & Aziz, K. (2015). Toward professional standards for media transparency in the United States: Comparison of perceptions of non-transparency in national vs. regional media. *Proceedings of the 18th Annual International Interdisciplinary Public Relations Research Conference* (pp. 406–429). Miami,

FL: University of Miami. [Top ethics paper]. Retrieved from http://iprrc.org/ proceedings/IPRRC18-Proceedings-1.pdf.

Tsetsura, K., & Grynko, A. (2009). An exploratory study of the media transparency in Ukraine. *Public Relations Journal*, *3*(2). Retrieved from www.prsa.org/SearchResults/download/6D-030205/0/An_Exploratory_ Study_of_the_Media_Transparency_in.

Tsetsura, K., & Kruckeberg, D. (2009). *Truth, public relations, and the mass media: A normative model to examine media opacity.* Paper presented at the Annual Meeting of the International Public Relations Research Conference, Miami, FL.

Tsetsura, K., & Luoma-aho, V. (2010). Innovative thinking or distortion of journalistic values? How the lack of trust creates non-transparency in the Russian media. *Ethical Space: The International Journal of Communication Ethics*, *7*(4), 30–38.

Zoch, L. M., & Molleda, J. C. (2006). Building a theoretical model of media relations using framing, information subsidies, and agenda-building. In C. H. Botan & V. Hazleton (Eds.), *Public relations theory II* (pp. 279–309). Mahwah, NJ: Lawrence Erlbaum.

6 Professional Communities against Media Bribery

- Purpose: This chapter discusses how professional communities around the world resist media bribery by generating discussions among those within these professional communities.
- Scope: Professionals in many parts of the world have a great opportunity to address media bribery as an unacceptable and unethical practice within the field because the field is still growing and transforming in many parts of the world. The need for conducting ethical public relations practices in different countries is on the shoulders of the practitioners who work in those countries and of those who introduce and educate practitioners about modern public relations practices.
- Method: This chapter uses examples from previous studies and the authors' reflections from discussions with professionals from throughout the world to demonstrate the transformative change of open discussions about media bribery practices.
- Results: The results of many discussions have shown that the vast majority of professional journalists and public relations practitioners throughout the world condemn media opacity and see this practice as a destroyer of goodwill and trust in societies.
- Recommendations: Members of professional communities must, themselves, call for the need for media transparency and must regulate how violations of this need must be addressed.
- Conclusions: New forms of media non-transparency bring additional challenges and warrant attention.

Today, public relations has become increasingly important because of the loss of a sense of physical community, which arises from new means of communication. Technology is driving this change, not just for the good in terms of globalization and connecting different communities, but also through undermining existing communities that are based on more traditional social mores by the sharing of more liberal, different ideas. Public relations is no longer about persuading individuals or being aligned with a corporation's goals, but about supporting communities. To undertake this evolving role, public relations professionals must not only have cultural, historical, and ideological knowledge about their own societies to perform their role, but must also possess broad experience of other societies, that is, they must have an understanding of global breadth and historical depth.

For any profession to exist and to be recognized as such, a body of literature, a prescribed education and accreditation/certification, and a code of ethics are essential. Public relations needs to be perceived as professional to ensure that its professionals (both practitioners and scholars) have the appropriate class (remuneration), status, and power and influence. This becomes especially important because communication technology is not just driving change, but is also introducing chaos (Kruckeberg & Tsetsura, 2008). The chaotic nature of today's fragmented society brings a qualitatively new understanding of the world to communication professionals. What a century ago had become national through communication is now inarguably global; what a century ago was a resegmentation of citizens into occupational and professional communities on a national scale has now arguably become a global fragmentation representing seemingly infinite perspectives on multiple issues; what a century ago was inverted from public to private has now become a confusing, threatening, and undoubtedly highly dangerous concoction, a re-inversion of what is private, which can become globally public at a keystroke, and what should be public, or transparent.

Thus, the changing landscape of today's communication is characterized by the following (Kruckeberg & Tsetsura, 2009):

- A loss of monopoly of knowledge by professional communicators to an immense number of purveyors who have access to the world audience via the Internet
- Seemingly infinite user-provided content
- Inexpensive and easily accessible electronic channels of communication
- Information that can emanate from any user (known or unknown, credible or not) to any consumer irrespective of time and space
- A rapid erosion and de-professionalization of journalism and arguably public relations

To attain a new approach to public relations practices, a seamless and integrated professional community needs to be established: practitioners, scholars, and students working together. In particular, scholars and practitioners of Eastern European countries must join in the global discussion and share their experiences. This is an exciting time for the field of public relations in Eastern Europe because professionals in these transitioning countries have an opportunity to build the field of public relations according to the professional standards they, themselves, identify in accordance with standards and experiences of professionals from throughout the world on one hand, and with historical, economical, and cultural particularities of their environments on the other hand (Tsetsura & Kruckeberg, 2009).

Despite differences, practitioners throughout the world have become increasingly alike as a global professional community because of how communication technology has affected global society. Communication technology has become the most influential and powerful intervening variable that simultaneously permits and encourages a global society through the compression of time and space, while paradoxically exacerbating social conflicts that are caused by the increased multiculturalism caused by globalization forces, both in the world-at-large and in its regions, nations, and localities. Thus, our global society remains divisive and fragmented in many ways.

Today, journalists and the media have lost their monopoly of knowledge. In the 1970s in the United States, mergers of media companies created citizens' fear of these companies' monopoly of knowledge. Nowadays, media companies increasingly provide only the channels of communication, and citizens provide much of the content and have great influence on news agendas. This loss of monopoly of content has an impact on the ethics of "professionalized" communication as well as the very concept of "news" (Kruckeberg & Tsetsura, 2009). Because communication has become inexpensive both to send and to receive, the role of journalism has become increasingly deprofessionalized: today everyone (technologically, at least) can become a journalist—eroding the professional role of the journalist.

In other words, "news" is no longer vetted, and traditional gatekeepers of information increasingly are being eliminated. The concept of news and its corresponding news values as they have evolved over the course of nearly two centuries are being diluted, if not dissolved. Much, if not most, of the content in the new media has become once again ideological with no attempt at fairness and objectivity according to the traditional concept of news and its news values. However, the plenitude of sources and their uneven credibility may be increasingly recognized as such by many consumers of this content. These new media may have reintroduced and reinforced a healthy skepticism about the integrity of media sources. Thus, the Internet may have done a great service to society in creating a healthy skepticism about the truthfulness of media, refocusing responsibility on the consumers of these media.

In the era of globalism and a growing fragmentation of the society, one also must question the continuing utility of the concept of segmented publics (plural) (Kruckeberg & Tsetsura, 2009; Kruckeberg & Vujnovic, 2010). Kruckeberg and Tsetsura (2009) have observed that infinite numbers of volatile "publics" worldwide can form immediately and unpredictably, and they can act seemingly chaotically and with unforeseen power. Thus, one must question the contemporary accuracy of practitioners' historic contention that public relations programs seldom will be effective if they are directed to a mass audience and that the costs of a campaign itself will be much greater because messages are directed to "nonpublics" as well as to identified and targeted strategic publics. In today's global environment that has compressed time and space and that has made the cost of communication inconsequentially inexpensive to provide and to receive and upon which to immediately act, it has become meaningless to identify "publics" (plural) and instead we should reassess the importance of a general public (Kruckeberg & Tsetsura, 2009; Kruckeberg & Vujnovic, 2010).

This re-evaluation of the concept of *a general public* is particularly important in light of contemporary communication technology that has become the most influential and powerful intervening variable, which simultaneously permits and encourages a global society through the compression of time and space. While paradoxically exacerbating social conflicts because of increased multiculturalism, communication technology not only (1) is allowing and is increasing the compression of time and space and (2) is making global communication unprohibitively inexpensive both to send and to receive, but also (3) has overwhelmed people with information and (4) has intermingled traditional vetted sources of information with user-generated content (UGC) that may be suspect in its source credibility as well as nontransparent in its agenda. With globalization and the compression of time and space and abundant and inexpensive interaction, it is difficult, if not impossible, to predict how publics will form, organize, and respond to organizational activities. The migration of people to online environments develops social interactions that have caught the attention of practitioners who see value in reaching out to stakeholders with the intent to build communities (Kruckeberg & Tsetsura, 2008; Kruckeberg & Vujnovic, 2010).

As communities convene globally on an ad hoc basis it has become more difficult to identify the "publics" and to build strategies to target *publics* and *the public* (Kruckeberg & Tsetsura, 2009). More appropriate is to see the corporation as operating in a larger social system in which it coexists and operates in harmony. Social media help create organic interaction between members of the public and organisations as well as with governments on all levels. Social media are the point of intersection between global and local, and the very idea that they are social will hopefully push organizations toward bridging participatory gaps and building communities, while maintaining good communication strategies. A move to an anthropological rather than quantitative approach is required to measure the outcomes of public relations that have dominated public relations scholarship and practice (Vujnovic & Kruckeberg, 2010).

Global communication influences organizations and their publics, and communication innovations make understanding global publics more urgent. Organizations that want to succeed in the global environment must recognize the strengths of the new social media that allow for building local awareness and local communities and linking them to the larger global context. The unpredictability of how and why humans organize allows organizations to influence messages as well as to be more watchful about what is said. This argument calls for redefining our understanding of public relations to include the multiplicity of communities and the presence of a "general public", which recognizes the complexity of contemporary global society and appreciates the threats to society at this macro level.

Eastern European scholars and practitioners must not only educate tomorrow's professionals, but must accept the responsibility to substantively contribute in the global arena in building relevant theories to propel the development of the field of public relations. And students must not only aspire to join this professional community in their future roles of educators and practitioners, but also must take every opportunity to best prepare for the unprecedented future challenges of this professionalized occupation. To achieve these recommendations, educators, practitioners, and students can and should join and be active in formal professional associations, such as the Russian public relations associations RASO and RASSO, and must actively participate in global discussions about public relations practice, scholarship, and education. This global professional community's members can and must make their unique contributions to public relations as this professionalized occupation continues to evolve into a unified body of knowledge and best practices worldwide.

Robinson (1966), in his book *Communication and Public Relations*, identified the core functions for any public relations practitioner, drawing on the contention that public relations is an applied social and behavioral science. To this day, these functions, with several unifying generalizations, regardless of application, can be considered as scientific principles in every sense of the word. These are:

- Understanding of communication: If you are to practice public relations, you must be able to communicate, with a theoretical understanding of the communication process.
- Understanding of attitude and behavioral change: To understand reasons behind people's attitudes toward you and your organization.
- Understanding of business administration: A background in management theory is extremely useful, as well as in financial and strategic management.
- To practice public relations, you must constantly receive reliable feedback so that you can intelligently shape and modify your programs. You must continually perform research to determine the attitudes and the less stable opinions that people have of your organization or client.

These principles are, indeed, true for both academia and practice today. To improve public relations education, many professional associations and organizations throughout the world are now actively engaged in collaboration with universities and college. One way to do so is to conduct high-profile, comprehensive research. Practitioners, together with academicians in North America, Asia, Easter Europe, and Latin America, engage in research to establish whether scholars and practitioners from these regions are finding their own voice, are following the footsteps of Western thinking in public relations, or are combining Western (particularly, US) thinking with local perspectives. They are also on the quest to identify the best ways for successful collaboration between academia and the industry and to showcase the best collaborative practices. For instance, the United States Commission on Public Relations Education has published significant papers on public relations education (for example, *Standards for a Master's Degree in Public Relations: Educating for Complexity*, 2012; *The Professional Bond*, 2006) and, under the auspices of the Global Alliance for Public Relations and Communication Management (and sponsored by the Public Relations Society of America Foundation), is attempting to identify the many different approaches to teaching public relations at colleges and universities throughout the world, with the intention of establishing minimum global standards for teaching public relations, taking into account culture and the multicultural reality of our modern societies as well as globalization (see the website of the Commission on Public Relations Education, www.commpred. org, and also the Global Body of Knowledge—Capabilities Framework Report of the Global Alliance for Public Relations and Communications Management, www.globalalliancepr.org/capabilitiesframeworks). Also, the Canadian Public Relations Association, together with its Education Council, has developed *Pathways to the Profession*, which includes curriculum standards, a framework for recognizing institutions, and a framework for an entry-level credential (www.cprs.ca/education/pathways.aspx). The PRSA's voluntary Certification in Education for Public Relations (CEPR) program reviews and endorses those academic programs that meet its standards in public relations education (Public Relations Student Society of America, 2016). Currently, 40 institutions have earned this certification. They include 37 undergraduate programs, four of which are in Argentina, Colombia, Peru and New Zealand; two master's programs, one of which is in Ireland; and an education program in Canada. They have received this certification by going through a rigorous application and certification process (http://prssa. prsa.org/about/certification).

Common in each of these examples is the adherence to excellence in public relations education within a professional community through the formal structure of professional associations. These associations must fully engage in the global discussion of public relations practice, scholarship, and education (each professional community, nationally, regionally, and globally) and must make its unique contributions to public relations as this professionalized occupation continues to evolve into a unified body of knowledge and best practices worldwide.

The next section of this chapter discusses recent research on media transparency in the United States.

Media Transparency in the United States

As the United States occupied the fifth place out of 33 ranks in the original index of media bribery (Kruckeberg & Tsetsura, 2003), few attempts were made to study media non-transparency in the country (Tsetsura & Aziz, 2015). One study separated responses of U.S. public relations practitioners and U.S. journalists from the global survey of media bribery to investigate what direct and indirect forms of media bribery in the USA might have affected media credibility in the USA (Tsetsura & Klyueva, 2010). The study found that U.S. communication professionals overwhelmingly disapprove of media bribery. But the results also showed the presence of various indirect media non-transparent practices in the United States. Advertising pressure was the most commonly spread practice (Tsetsura & Klyueva, 2010). The current trends to embrace native advertising and brand journalism by many U.S. media outlets may further increase the belief among U.S. communicators that the media can still be credible even if it is influenced by news sources and advertisers.

To understand whether media non-transparent practices are perceived as acceptable or ethical in the United States, one should first examine a professional code of ethical standards agreed upon by the country's professionals (Tsetsura & Kruckeberg, 2009). PRSA is the largest professional association of public relations practitioners in the USA and thus is a logical choice to start an investigation. The PRSA code of ethics sets the industry standards for professional practice in the field of public relations (Public Relations Society of America, 2016). The organization requires members to pledge to the code of ethics, and membership can be revoked if professionals do not abide (although this rarely happens, if ever). The code has several core values, including advocacy, honesty, loyalty, professional development, and objectivity. In addition to these core values, the code calls for practitioners to avoid conflicts of interest, promote healthy and fair competition, protect confidential information, and work to strengthen the public's trust of public relations. In addition to the code, PRSA's Board of Ethics and Professional Standards periodically addresses current issues and challenges facing public relations, such as pay-for-play journalism.

Although having a code of ethics is a right step toward media transparency in the United States, should pay-for-play journalism only cover direct media bribery? If not, what should be defined as indirect bribery, and how can PRSA leaders discuss these issues with the professional community in the United States? Do practitioners in this country face direct or indirect media bribery requests? Today, PRSA does not have a clear answer to these questions. With the results of the new study of media bribery in the USA, PRSA's Board of Ethics and Professional Standards received the opportunity to look at "pay-for-play journalism" in a more vigorous way (Tsetsura & Aziz, 2015). Tsetsura and Aziz (2015) conducted a survey of PRSA members in the USA. They found that, overall, direct forms of media bribery are not widespread in the USA. However, according to respondents in this study, an indirect form of bribery, that is, advertising pressure, occurred statistically significantly more at local/regional levels. This finding was consistent with previous media transparency research (Tsetsura, 2005; Klyueva & Tsetsura, 2010, 2011). The most frequently reported form of indirect media bribery (a journalist who has benefited from a product or service) was more frequently disclosed in national media outlets than local/regional ones (Tsetsura & Aziz, 2015). Additionally, local/regional media in the United States face financial and advertising pressures (a form of indirect media bribery) more frequently than national media.

The authors of this study suggested adding a section to the PRSA Member Code of Ethics that defines direct and indirect media bribery as well as provides practical guidelines to help with the decision-making process in light of the latest trend toward native advertising in the media. Such guidelines might help PRSA and other professional associations and organizations generate discussions about new kinds of media non-transparency that are closely related to native advertising.

Native Advertising[1]

Native advertising (or content marketing) is an emerging "buzzword". As the Interactive Advertising Bureau (IAB) (2016) states, we are far from an agreed-upon definition of what native advertising is. Native advertising can be defined as a way for companies and marketers to engage with consumers in a new way online. The IAB (2016) argued that advertisers and publishers use native advertising to deliver "paid ads that are so cohesive with the page content, assimilated into the design, and consistent with the platform behavior that the viewer simply feels that they belong" there (p. 3).

The IAB (2016) identified six types of native advertising: (1) in-feed units (appear on Facebook as part of one's newsfeed); (2) paid search units (appear as Google search results); (3) recommendation widgets; (4) promoted listings (seen on Amazon); (5) in-ad native element units;

---

1 The authors would like to recognize former graduate assistant Kelsie Aziz as a co-author of this section of the chapter.

and (6) custom, or "can't be contained" (as seen on Tumblr, Spotify, and Pandora). Google, Facebook, and Amazon are not the only big names to introduce native advertising on their websites. In early 2014, *The New York Times* debuted native advertising on their newly redesigned website, with Dell as the first advertiser (Sebastian, 2014).

Media ethics and transparency scholars and practitioners should continue to pay special attention to native advertising and its ethical and transparency implications. As the IAB (2016) noted, native advertising is *cohesive* with the normal page content and *assimilated* into the design. However, nowhere in that description does the IAB argue that this advertising should be clearly marked as such.

This transparency issue is one that *Forbes* writer Dvorkin (2014) discussed; Dvorkin argued that "both consumer and marketer require equal parts transparency". Castillo (2014) reported that BuzzFeed decided to change its native advertising label to clearly mark content by placing a bright yellow box next to it containing the words "promoted by". Previously, BuzzFeed marked its native advertising with the words "presented by" in a light yellow box, which some argued was hard to see on mobile devices. *The New York Times*, on the other hand, which, as discussed, has an extensive ethics policy, clearly marks its new native advertising section. When a consumer clicks on the "paid posts" on the Times websites, they are redirected to a site, paidpost.nytimes. com, and there are also additional disclaimers on the page (Sebastian, 2014). However, social media sites, such as Instagram and Facebook, are much more subtle when labeling their native advertising (Castillo, 2014).

This native advertising phenomenon is one that seems to be picking up in popularity among public relations, journalists, and advertisers alike. The Native Advertising Summit (NAS), for example, is the "premier conference dedicated to defining and discussing the future of native advertising" (Eventifier, 2014). In 2013, the NAS held four sold-out conferences across the United States. The next NAS summit was held in July 2014 in San Francisco and included high profile speakers from *The New York Times*, *USA Today*, and even Pinterest.

However, it is important that public relations professionals and journalists are mindful of the transparency implications of native advertising. Is subtly including the word "promoted" above the advertisement enough? Or, does it need to be boldly marked, such as on some news website? Furthermore, public relations professionals in the United States need to understand how they might be able to use native advertising to help disseminate messages to their publics in a new, innovative way, while also doing so ethically.

Examination of the current media transparency in the USA will help to investigate native advertising through a media transparency lens in the future. Lack of agreed-upon professional guidelines on how media should publish and label native advertising might create ambiguity about the intentions of the message and contribute to a decrease in the legitimacy of the media and distrust in society (Tolvanen, Olkkonen, & Luoma-aho, 2013). There is also a potential for native advertising to become a new form of indirect media bribery. Therefore, ambiguity of native advertising should be addressed, especially because this new phenomenon is an innovative and different way to connect with audiences. If organizations want to ethically publish native advertising in the media, they must think about how non-transparency will affect future legitimacy and trust if these messages are not clearly labeled as advertisements. Already, there might be double standards for publishing native advertising, as we have observed with news media and BuzzFeed. For public relations scholars and practitioners, such ambiguity presents an interesting and relevant new way to study media transparency and indirect media bribery in the United States.

References

Canadian Public Relations Society. *Pathways to the profession—An overview: A new relationship for CPRS and educators*. Toronto, Ontario, Canada.

Castillo, M. (2014, May 30). BuzzFeed changes labels on promoted content: Sponsored material gets simple yet clear design. *AdWeek Online: Technology*. Retrieved from www.adweek.com/news/technology/buzzfeed-changes-labels-promoted-content-158060.

Dvorkin, L. (2014, March 25). Inside Forbes: 10 battlegrounds to watch as native advertising marches on. *Forbes Online*. Retrieved from www.forbes.com/sites/lewisdvorkin/2014/03/25/inside-forbes-10-battlegrounds-to-watch-as-native-advertising-marches-on/.

Eventifier. (2014, July 22). Native Advertising Summit. Retrieved from http://eventifier.com/event/nas2014/.

Global Alliance for Public Relations and Communication Management. (2015, July). "The standard" to practice public relations and communication management. Lugano, Switzerland. Global Alliance for Public Relations and Communication Management.

Interactive Advertising Bureau (2016). Native advertising. Web article. Retrieved from www.iab.com/wp-content/uploads/2015/06/IAB-Native-Advertising-Playbook2.pdf.

Klyueva, A., & Tsetsura, K. (2011). News from the Urals with love and payment: The first look at non-transparent media practices in the Urals Federal District of Russia. *Russian Journal of Communication, 4*(1/2), 72–93.

Klyueva, A., & Tsetsura, K. (2010). Media non-transparency research: A case of Romania. *Public Relations Journal, 4*(4). Retrieved from www.prsa.org/Intelligence/PRJournal/Documents/2010FallKlyuevaTsetsura.pdf.

Kruckeberg, D., & Tsetsura, K. (November, 2009). *The role of public relations and technology in global society*. Keynote presentation at the International Anniversary Journalism Conference, Journalism School, University of Bucharest, Bucharest, Romania.

Kruckeberg, D., & Tsetsura, K. (2008). The Chicago school in the global community: Concept explication for communication theories and practices. *Asian Communication Research, 5,* 9–30. [Lead article]

Kruckeberg, D., & Tsetsura, K. (2003). International index of bribery for news coverage. *Institute for Public Relations Report: International Research.* Retrieved from www.instituteforpr.org/bribery-news-coverage-2003/.

Kruckeberg, D., & Vujnovic, M. (2010). The death of the concept of "publics" (plural) in 21st century public relations. *International Journal of Strategic Communication, 4,* 1–9.

The Professional Bond (2006, November). New York: Commission on Public Relations Education.

Public Relations Society of America. (2016). Public Relations Society of America member code of ethics. New York: Public Relations Society of America.

Public Relations Student Society of America. (2016). PR program certification. New York: Public Relations Society of America.

Robinson, E. J. (1966). Communication and public relations. Columbus, OH: Charles E. Merrill Publishing Co.

Sebastian, M. (2014, January 08). Five things to know about The New York Times' new native ads. *Advertising Age.* Retrieved from http://adage.com/article/media/york-times-debuts-native-ad-units-dell/290973/.

Standards for a master's degree in public relations: Educating for Complexity (2012, October). New York: Commission on Public Relations Education.

Tolvanen, K., Olkkonen, L., & Luoma-aho, V. (2013). The legitimacy of the media industry—what do advertisers expect? *Journal of Media Business Studies, 10*(4), 17–38.

Tsetsura, K. (2005). Bribery for news coverage: Research in Poland. *Institute for Public Relations Online: International Research.* Retrieved from www.instituteforpr.org/research_single/bribery_for_news/.

Tsetsura, K., & Aziz, K. (2015). Toward professional standards for media transparency in the United States: Comparison of perceptions of non-transparency in national vs. regional media. *Proceedings of the 18th Annual International Interdisciplinary Public Relations Research Conference* (pp. 406–429). Miami, FL: University of Miami [Top ethics paper]. Retrieved from http://iprrc.org/proceedings/IPRRC18-Proceedings-1.pdf.

Tsetsura, K., & Klyueva, A. (2010). Ethicality of media opacity as a predictor of acceptance of non-transparent media practices among the Romanian media professionals. *Proceedings of the 13th International Interdisciplinary Public Relations Research Conference* (p. 696). Miami, FL: University of Miami. Retrieved from www.instituteforpr.org/wp-content/uploads/IPRRC_13_Proceedings.pdf [named one of the Top Five Papers Published in *PR Journal* in 2009].

Tsetsura, K., & Kruckeberg, D. (2009). Corporate reputation: Beyond measurement. *Public Relations Journal, 3*(3). Retrieved from www.prsa.org/SearchResults/download/6D-030303/0/Corporate_Reputation_Beyond_Measurement?.

Vujnovic, M., & Kruckeberg, D. (2010). The local, national, and global challenges of public relations: A call for an anthropological approach to practicing public relations. In R. L. Heath (Ed.), *Handbook of Public Relations, 2nd edition* (pp. 671–678). Thousand Oaks, CA: Sage Publications, Inc.

7 A Normative Theory of Media Bribery

- Purpose: To summarize the arguments in this book and to make recommendations to combat hidden influences in news media worldwide.
- Scope: To summarize the validity, while recognizing the futility, of addressing news media opacity as an ethical issue.
- Method: To make concluding arguments for an "ideal state" of transparency by and among the news media and the discrete professional communities of journalists and public relations practitioners, an "ideal state" that should be expected and demanded by the consumers of news media, that is, citizens and marketplace consumers.
- Results: Journalists and their news media as well as public relations practitioners will increasingly accept the "ideal state" of transparency in the news media; citizens and marketplace consumers, who are the consumer stakeholders of these news media, will increasingly demand this "ideal state".
- Recommendations: The reader should proactively encourage news media transparency in his or her role and relationship with the news media, whether as a journalist, a public relations practitioner, or as a citizen and marketplace consumer.
- Conclusions: That media opacity must be combated by publicly declared and universally adhered-to ethical standards (1) that require transparency within the professional communities of public relations practitioners and journalists and their news media and (2) that must be demanded by stakeholders, that is, citizens and marketplace consumers.

News Media Opacity That Allows Hidden Influences Is Ubiquitous Throughout the World

This book began with the alarming statement that consumers of news throughout the world are not being told the truth because news media opacity has allowed hidden influences to alter what we consume as "news".

This opacity compromises these news media's publicly perceived role to present news and other information based on these gatekeepers' perception of this information's truth. We defined *news media opacity* as a conscious lack of *news media transparency*, the latter in which no hidden influences exist in the process of gathering/disseminating news and other information that is presented as truth or in which these influences have been clearly identified in the end-product in the media. *Hidden influences* include inducements that may be proffered by public relations practitioners or the solicitation of these inducements that may be demanded by news media or their representatives; these inducements may include monetary and non-monetary payments, free products or services, or punishments, for example, the threat or the actual withdrawal of advertising. Importantly, we did not include in these hidden influences those barriers to truth in which journalists and their news media are not complicit, for example when journalists and their news media are victims to demands for control from oppressive governments, restrictive laws, or the threat of physical harm.

Our definition of *truth* in the news media is accurate, complete, and unbiased information that has been gathered and verified conscientiously and competently and that is presented fairly and in good faith by those who are attempting to achieve the ideal of objectivity with complete transparency in gathering, analyzing, and presenting this information. This definition acknowledges that a well-intentioned communicator who believes that he or she is telling the truth may in fact be wrong, but it is the truth as the communicator believed it to be at the time and that had been disseminated in good faith. We defined truth as such because this definition allows us to restrict our discussion solely to ethical questions related to truth as it is disseminated in the news media.

We did not contend that most news media blatantly and pervasively disseminate information that is a lie, which we defined as information that the communicator knows to be false that is presented with the intent to deceive and/or mislead. Rather, citizens and marketplace consumers simply are not being told the "whole truth" by some journalists and their news media throughout much of the world because of hidden influences. Our research has revealed that what we call incomplete truth exists in the news media to greater or lesser extents worldwide. We defined *incomplete truth* as news and other information that is being presented as truth that may be by-and-large accurate, but in which the news gatherer/disseminator has intentionally omitted contextualizing information or has purposely failed to identify influences that have altered the presentation of this information with the outcome of deceiving and/or misleading the consumers of this news.

Together with differing cultures, histories, and prevailing ideologies throughout the world that influence news media opacity, the proliferation of incomplete truth resulting from hidden influences that can occur because of news media opacity is exacerbated by today's changing business models of news media that are responding to people's use of new forms of communication technology. We argue for the elimination of these hidden influences in the news media's news gathering/dissemination process and call for transparency by journalists and public relations practitioners in their relationship to one another as they perform their discrete, but complementary, roles in society. The trust of citizens and marketplace consumers is the desired outcome in our call for the elimination of incomplete truth in the news media worldwide. *Trust* in this book is defined as citizens and marketplace consumers' belief in the truth of the news that is disseminated in the news media. We concur with the conclusion of Valentini and Kruckeberg (2011), who argued:

> (T)rust can only exist where it is deserved, i.e. such trust cannot be betrayed. A requisite of trust is the reasonable prediction and anticipation of an action by an actor based on that actor's prior behavior and other communication. (p. 101)

Indeed, we vehemently argue that the news media's universal societal role is to present the truth. We define news media as organizations that disseminate news and other information to a general audience through channels of communication that include newspapers, radio and television stations, the Internet and its websites, and various forms of social media.

Despite today's sea of readily available and free or inconsequentially inexpensive information, much of which is presented as news or at least is being interpreted as news, we believe that citizens and marketplace consumers worldwide—irrespective of their indigenous cultures, histories, and prevailing ideologies—will continue to need professional journalists and their news media as this book has defined them to help set the news agenda, to grade the news, and to provide informed and impartial interpretation of current events as well as to help citizens and marketplace consumers make informed life decisions. However, if news media opacity hides myriad influences that result in incomplete truth, journalists and their news media are not fulfilling this role and do not deserve the trust of citizens and marketplace consumers.

News Media Opacity Is Unquestionably an Ethical Issue

We have argued that opacity in the news gathering/dissemination process is a significant threat to people worldwide as citizens and as marketplace consumers, all of whom need and undoubtedly want truth to make the best life decisions. This should be especially obvious in societies that claim to be democratic as well as civil and humane, but we argue that truth through media transparency is requisite in all societies. Influences that are hidden through news media opacity alter what we consume as "news", creating incomplete truth that can only be regarded as an insidious attempt to inappropriately and unethically manipulate and control people that must be viewed as a threat to citizens and marketplace consumers as well as to society at large. When public relations practitioners pay bribes for their media releases to be disseminated in the news media or when other hidden influences alter the information that people consume as "news", a betrayal of trust occurs because journalists and their news media are promoting the illusion among consumers that the news that journalists have gathered and that the news media have disseminated is accurate, complete, and unbiased.

Thus, we conclude that news media opacity that hides incomplete truth clearly and unquestionably is an ethical issue; we argue that news media transparency should be a universal requisite. Thereby, news media opacity that hides incomplete truth is a professional ethical transgression against what we argue is a universal right to truth from the news media, which societal institution citizens and marketplace consumers should be able to trust. Certainly in no culture or situation can journalists and their news media declare that they deserve trust when news media opacity hides influences in the news gathering/dissemination process that result in incomplete truth. We further argue that journalists and their news media are the primary agents that must assume ultimate ethical responsibility and accountability for the quality and integrity of their product, the news. Nevertheless, other actors share ethical responsibility and accountability to assure news media transparency, specifically public relations practitioners as a professional community and citizens and marketplace consumers as stakeholders.

The Need for News Media Transparency Is Universal

To re-emphasize, we believe that the requisite for news media transparency is universal, that is, news media transparency should be the norm for all indigenous societies worldwide and should be applicable to all professional journalists and their news media globally. That said, we recognize that worldwide consensus about news media transparency and any global mandate opposing news media opacity is unlikely—certainly in the near future in which a globalized world nevertheless remains highly multicultural. This is not only because of disparate ethical perspectives worldwide, but also because incomplete truth that results from these hidden influences that are made possible through media opacity are highly profitable and advantageous to some journalists, their news media, and public relations practitioners. One can predict that these journalists, their news media, and public relations practitioners' sense of moral outrage will be lacking and that their resistance to news media opacity will be less than enthusiastic; furthermore, news media opacity that hides influences resulting in incomplete truth often either is unknown or is tacitly accepted by citizens and marketplace consumers. Indeed, evidence presented in the preceding chapters of this book suggests that media bribery and other hidden influences occur often and with considerable impunity worldwide.

Thus, with resignation, the authors of this book believe that the need for ethically desirable media transparency will more likely become universally accepted—or at least more highly valued—by framing news media transparency as having both increased intrinsic and, thereby, economic value. Then, truth through news media transparency can be positioned and marketed effectively through branding and publicly declared codes of ethics. While these may first appear to be superficial and inadequate means to address the problem of incomplete truth made possible through hidden influences resulting from media opacity, such campaigns nevertheless can be quite effective and, regrettably, may be the only viable means to address this ethical problem globally. Frankly, few other options exist short of legal sanctions, which should not be endorsed because of their considerable potential for abuse, that is, laws requiring media transparency can easily create an oppressive regulatory environment that is antithetical to what we are seeking as an ethical outcome. These efforts will also help address other problems that are arising as the news media attempt to compete in the sea of information that now exists for millions of people throughout the world through the Internet and its social media. Our specific recommendations follow.

How It Used to Be

News Media: A century ago in the United States and to varying extents elsewhere throughout the world, people relied on newspapers for their news. Wire services and major newspapers that could afford news correspondents provided national and international news at varying levels. The advent of radio, with a highly limited band spectrum, and then television with three major networks and their local affiliates, provided additional channels of communication that allowed news media to provide, not only more news, but also additional news media choices. Of course, news media required considerable resources to gather and to disseminate their product, and choices of news media for citizens and marketplace consumers remained highly limited. An individual could subscribe to his or her local newspaper as well as a regional newspaper and perhaps one of the few national newspapers; could listen to a local or regional radio station; and could view both local and national news on his or her television set. A more demanding consumer of the news could subscribe to additional newspapers, of course at an escalating cost, and certainly was welcome to visit his or her public library to peruse a still wider range of newspapers. News media had a strong monopoly of knowledge in an era in which relatively few news media existed in the limited channels of communication that had evolved. Nevertheless in the United States and elsewhere in the world, sufficient market competition assured overall high quality of news—although, beginning in the 1970s, cities began losing competing newspapers and concerns were being raised about newspaper chains' concentrated control of large numbers of newspapers. But, as our research has suggested, media opacity certainly was allowing hidden influences in the gathering and dissemination of news during an era in which media transparency was generally assumed.

Journalists: Primarily because of First Amendment rights, anyone in the United States legally could assume the role of a journalist regardless of any professional credentials to do so; of course, such would be a reality only given that individual's economic resources to do so, that is, would a journalistic hopeful have available channels of communication to disseminate his or her journalistic offerings? Even a letter to the editor would be vetted by gatekeepers, and entry to dissemination of news and other information in the mass media—including the news media—remained highly inaccessible to most citizens. Journalists were highly professionalized; those who were competitive in seeking professional positions as journalists in the news media would generally have a prescribed education in journalism's professional body of knowledge as well as a mastery of professional skills and abilities. Such an education was usually accompanied by these journalists' understanding of the professionally agreed-upon role of news media in a free and democratic society, adherence to and performance according to generally accepted news values, and a shared consensus about professional ethics; of course in many other countries throughout the world, somewhat different knowledge, skills, and abilities—as well as agreed-upon news values and professional ethics—might be prerequisite to what sometimes would be required professional licensure according to a country's prevailing press systems and media laws.

Regardless, journalism was a highly professionalized occupation that imposed relatively high barriers to entry for those wanting to compete for the limited number of positions in the finite number of news media that competed with one another using relatively few channels of communication; without proper credentials, one could not realistically become a member of this exclusive community of professional journalists.

Public Relations Practitioners: Public relations likewise became increasingly professionalized throughout its relatively short history; for much of its existence, practitioners performed extensively, oftentimes primarily, in news media relations, that is, by pitching story ideas to journalists, by placing news media releases, as well as by volunteering as willing sources or source facilitators for journalists. If public relations practitioners did not adhere to the professional values and ethics of journalists, or if they considered these values and ethics to be detrimental to their clients' promotional interests, practitioners knew that they at least would have to accommodate those values and ethics to be successful in their efforts on behalf of their clients in the dissemination of media releases. Again, as our research suggests, some practitioners would be willingly complicit in exploiting media opacity to publicize incomplete truth.

Citizens and Marketplace Consumers: Citizens and marketplace consumers throughout this period of time were largely dependent on the limited number of news media and their journalists for news because of these news media's monopoly of knowledge; nevertheless, such consumers of news could be reasonably complacent in this environment; in the United States as well as in many other countries, sufficient competition existed to assure the basic fulfillment of the news media's societal role. If citizens perhaps poorly understood the role and overall importance of the news media, they nevertheless generally would respect professional journalists and their news media that gathered and disseminated the news. Public relations undoubtedly was even less understood, and oftentimes invisible, to citizens and marketplace consumers because those practitioners who sought news media placement of their media releases had to fulfill the professional requirements of the journalists who were the gatekeepers. With perhaps only a rudimentary understanding of the role of the news media, maybe learned only in a high school civics class, citizens nevertheless not only respected, but also trusted, journalists and their news media. Again, as our research suggests, this trust may at times have been misplaced because of the incomplete truths and media opacity that this book has described.

How News Media Are Today

Of course, this short contemporary history of the evolution of the news media, their journalists, public relations practitioners, and the assumptions about the news media by citizens and marketplace consumers is oversimplified; however, it is sufficient to contrast that media environment to what is happening today. For the news media, the compression of time and space certainly has allowed increased, and arguably better, news coverage, often with far less expense in gathering the news and less expense in disseminating this news through new channels of communication. Even when restricted to what this book defines as the news media, the amount of news that is being gathered has become overwhelming, to a great extent because of easy and inexpensive access to sources of information as well as to increased news media partnerships; however, more dramatically and ultimately more significantly, the dissemination of this news is immense, in great part because new channels of communication are both inexpensive and easily accessible for consumers of the news: citizens and marketplace consumers have access to an immense amount of news from an incredible range of news media choices.

However, these news media have lost their monopoly of knowledge because entry to channels of communication is accessible to virtually everyone, meaning that vetted news that is being provided by these news media has been intermingled with—and oftentimes is perceived as indistinguishable from—content that is deservedly suspect in its source credibility and nontransparent in its agenda. Simply, news media no longer must compete only with one another using limited and highly expensive channels of communication, that is, with a relatively small number of news media organizations that not only had historically shared a monopoly of knowledge, but also that had shared news values and had employed journalists who shared professional news values and ethics; now, these news media must compete for consumers of the news with infinite sources of information, much of which is labeled as news and which is equally as inexpensive and as easily available to citizens and marketplace consumers whom the news media want to purchase their product, the news. Also lost to today's news media is their traditional agenda-setting role, which has become increasingly eroded and reactive because of the influence of the immense amount of other readily available information—with news agendas becoming increasingly determined by non-journalist contributors to the Internet and its social media. In this communication technology climate, it has become increasingly difficult, indeed impossible, for news media to position themselves as the sole gatherers and disseminators of news and to distinguish themselves exclusively as such in the sea of available information from which consumers have to choose. It becomes difficult to market their product, news, when a surfeit of information that is proffered and interpreted to be news is available from an immense number of sources.

Professional journalists likewise have suffered greatly in today's news media environment, and not only because of diminishing employment opportunities due to the continually downsizing of news media that are becoming less and less profitable and that appear increasingly not to be sustainable. We have argued that journalists' universal role remains to provide *truth* as this book has defined it; indeed, journalists' ability to gather and to disseminate this truth through the news media is what gives their professional occupation and the news media critical importance and essential roles in modern society. However, this role is becoming increasingly underappreciated, if even understood, by today's citizens and marketplace consumers who are overwhelmed by information choices and who increasingly appear to be lacking sufficient discernment to evaluate the relative worth of these available choices.

Barriers to entry to become a journalist have been removed, allowing anyone to perform the role of a journalist, regardless of that person's competence, professional and educational credentials, or adherence to—or even knowledge of—professionally agreed-upon journalistic ethics. While such a self-declared ipso facto practicing journalist may not be competitive in securing a job in the news media, he or she can easily and inexpensively compete in gathering and disseminating news because that individual does not require a printing press or a radio or television station and does not have to overcome other resource barriers to entry—essentially deprofessionalizing the concept of journalism because an individual can practice what was a professional occupation regardless of his or her knowledge of professional practices and ethical values and with little or no knowledge and respect for the concepts of news and news values.

As a result, these concepts of news and news values have become fluid and amorphous and oftentimes ideological, if not propagandistic. This deprofessionalization of journalism has resulted in professional journalists' lack of employment opportunities in the news media, in the demoralization of journalists, and in a drastically reduced number of students who are planning careers as journalists when they realize that any blogger or "participatory journalist" can claim membership in this professional community and, more importantly, has easy and inexpensive—in fact equal—access to potential consumers of his or her product. A democratization of journalism, which in some respects must be argued as having a functional value in a free and democratic society, nevertheless has deprofessionalized an occupation that previously had high barriers to entry; this is somewhat analogous to everyone being able to practice medicine regardless of competence, professional and educational credentials, or adherence to or—even knowledge of—professionally agreed-upon medical ethics, accompanied by consumers' inability to discern any difference between a credentialed physician and a person portending to be qualified to perform an appendectomy. Professional journalists working for news media have not become less professional, but what they do as professionals is being deprofessionalized because it is being done increasingly by nonprofessionals.

Public relations, likewise, had become increasingly professionalized throughout its relatively short history; for a considerable length of time, practitioners concerned themselves greatly, oftentimes primarily, with media relations, that is, with their relationships with the news media to which they pitched story ideas, attempted to place news media releases, and volunteered to serve as sources or facilitators for their clients' sources for news. Today, public relations practitioners and their organizations need the news media far less than in the past, in great part because they can easily and inexpensively reach their publics without the gatekeeping news media that enforces professional journalistic standards. Indeed, public relations practitioners increasingly are using their participation in the social media as a primary means to communicate with their publics.

Citizens and marketplace consumers unquestionably have benefited in many ways in this contemporary media environment. They have enjoyed free or inexpensive and easily accessible news in sufficient amounts to satisfy any desire for news that is available from myriad sources that can provide multiple perspectives. Also, citizens and marketplace consumers can access immense amounts of information directly from non-news media sources, because they are no longer held hostage to the news media's monopoly of knowledge or to the news media's traditional agenda-setting role. Because journalism has become democratized, some citizens and marketplace consumers have taken the opportunity to become ipso facto journalists. At some level, regardless of any professional credentials or any sense of news values and ethics, they can share in the power of professional journalists to inform and, as they wish, to attempt to form public opinion—no printing press, radio, or television station is required to communicate with mass audiences.

While this may be desirable in some respects, and certainly conducive to participatory democracy as well as beneficial in supporting social initiatives that many would find to be positive, for example, Arab Spring, significant dangers nevertheless exist in such a media environment. The greatest danger is not everyone's ability to disseminate information easily and inexpensively; restrictions on doing so would be anathema to participatory democracy. Rather, the danger lies in citizens and marketplace consumers' inability to discern the difference between such information and the product of news media and their professional journalists. One can readily argue that *The Wall Street Journal, The New York Times, The Washington Post,* and *The Times of London* are as credible online as these venerable news media are with their by-and-large identical content in newsprint. A discerning reader recognizes and appreciates the online content of *The Financial Times*, not confusing it with their friends' entries to Facebook, the information that was posted by those on Twitter, or whatever appears first in their Google search.

Increasingly, however, this may be a distinction that can be lost by many citizens and marketplace consumers in the sea of information that includes, not only truth from impeccable news media, but also incomplete truth and lies from questionable, if not suspect, sources. People holding a paper copy of *The New York Times* know what they are reading; however, the identity and credibility of such news media can be lost on goodly numbers of people surfing the Internet; what on their computer screens can appear as vetted news from that venerable newspaper is intermingled moments later—and oftentimes is perceived as indistinguishable—with content that may be suspect in its source credibility and nontransparent in its agenda.

Much has changed from the time when someone would say, "I read it in the newspaper", to today's, "I saw it on the Internet". Indeed, one of the authors of this book was on a local NPR radio program a few years ago in which the demise of newspapers was being discussed. A listener, who apparently was sufficiently erudite to listen to NPR, tweeted during the program that she got all of her news from Twitter. One must question how many people who say that they are getting their news online are obtaining this news from what this book defines as the news media; one must further ponder the implications of information on the Internet that may be truth as it is defined in this book, but much of which is more likely to be incomplete truth or lies. Not for all consumers of the overwhelming amount of content that is being communicated online does a healthy mistrust exist.

The Internet, despite its many benefits for humankind, has become more than just an additional channel of communication for news media and an opportunity to practice participatory democracy at a grassroots level. The Internet has seriously jeopardized the news media, which institution this book argues is essential to society and which will become increasingly essential in a globalized world. The fragmentation of mass audiences that previously were captive to fewer news media choices has played havoc with the business plans of news media, in good part by greatly increasing competition for advertising revenue by Internet-based organizations. A typical situation is that of the Guardian Media Group, whose chief executive in June 2011 declared a drastic cost reduction over a five-year period of time for that major United Kingdom newspaper, including "significant" job cuts, pagination reduction, redesigns, and a shift to that newspaper's website for editorial and financial investment. *The Financial Times* (Davoudi & Fenton, 2011) reported:

Like most media businesses, Guardian News & Media (GNM), the core division of GMG which publishes the flagship newspaper, has been hit by an unprecedented decline in advertising markets and the migration of readers to the internet. (p. 17)

This chief executive said he saw no let-up in the structural decline in print; he declared that there was no plan to discontinue print newspapers in five years, but market conditions could change that. United Kingdom readers have been migrating to the Internet, for which *The Financial Times* and *The Times* requires paid subscriptions; however, many other newspapers provide this news free of charge.

News media organizations increasingly are becoming victims of the Internet-focused marketplace, raising the question whether market conditions should be allowed to diminish or to eliminate what this book argues is an essential institution for society, that is, the news media, and an essential professional occupation, that is, journalism. Can global society afford to have the concept of news and its corresponding news values diluted by the infinite surfeit of information now available to billions of people worldwide? Our answer is no! Once again, as Kruckeberg and Tsetsura (2004) predicted:

> It seems almost certain that an overwhelming majority of people will continue to rely on journalists as experts and on news media...to gather and to report the news. This majority will depend on the gatekeepers of an established press to set news agenda, to grade news, and to provide informed comment about current events. (p. 89)

Simply, people do not have the time in their lives or, in most cases, the professional abilities to become their own journalists, mining immense amounts of information that is comprised, not only of truth, but much of which is incomplete truth and lies, to make the best life decisions as citizens and marketplace consumers. Global society needs the news media as this book defines this societal institution as well as a robust professional community of journalists who have a prescribed education in journalism's professional body of knowledge as well as a mastery of professional skills and abilities—accompanied by these journalists' understanding of the role of news media in a free and democratic society, adherence to and performance according to generally accepted news values, and a shared consensus about professional ethics.

The news media as this book has defined them have continuing, and we argue increasing, relevance in an era in which social media have allowed infinite numbers of messages to be sent from myriad sources using inexpensive channels of communication without any constraints of time and space. We argue that longstanding professional journalism practices and ethical values have not become passé; established concepts of news and news values continue to have meaning; and the agenda-setting role of the news media should not be allowed to become eroded. News must continue to be vetted by gatekeepers, and the news media must not be allowed to lose their identity and their influence.

Conclusions and Recommendations

We argue that news media transparency, which is a requisite to truth, is clearly an ethical imperative globally—regardless of indigenous cultures, histories, and ideologies throughout the world. However, the authors of this book recognize with resignation that worldwide consensus about news media transparency and any global mandate opposing news media opacity is highly unlikely because of disparate ethical perspectives worldwide and because incomplete truth that results from hidden influences that are made possible through media opacity are highly profitable and advantageous to some journalists, their news media, and public relations practitioners.

Thus, to achieve the ethical goal that we seek, we base our recommendations for media transparency on the greater intrinsic value of news that is gathered by professional journalists and disseminated by their news media as they have been defined in this book. Who will deny that truth has more intrinsic value than incomplete truth and lies? And this greater intrinsic value adds greater economic value to news media's product, the news. While news media and their professional journalists have irretrievably lost their monopoly of knowledge that had created their market strength in an era when these mass media were finite in number and their content was provided by an elite group of professional journalists, they can remain competitive in the marketplace because they gather and disseminate truth, not incomplete truth and lies.

Truth through news media transparency can be positioned and marketed effectively through branding and publicly declared codes of ethics. Trust of citizens and marketplace consumers will result. However, this trust must be deserved, and the research that was reported in this book suggests that such trust of the news media and their journalists may not always be deserved throughout much of the world. Media opacity must be eliminated, because truth that creates trust is all that can differentiate the news media in the twenty-first century from everything else in today's channels of communication, in particular the Internet.

Intrinsic value must be translated into perceived economic value to safeguard the news media as an essential societal institution. Perhaps with some irony, a massive public relations campaign is needed from the news media and their journalists. News media collectively worldwide must proactively identify, explain, and justify to citizens and marketplace consumers the need for truth as defined in this book and must publicize and expose the proliferation of incomplete truth that is disseminated—distinguishing themselves from these incomplete truths through their declared media transparency. Journalists through their professional associations must aggressively explain journalistic professionalism and its values and what constitutes journalism education and the mastery of requisite professional skills and abilities. Journalists as professionals must emphasize the essential role of news media in a free and democratic society and must help to educate citizens and marketplace consumers about news values and professional ethics. Public relations practitioners must likewise declare and enforce the ethics of their own professional community and must publicly support the ethics of journalists. Citizens and marketplace consumers must be more appreciative of the news media and its essential role in society, they must demand truth from transparent news media, and they must support the news media as consumer stakeholders. Society as a whole needs to continually examine the immense changes that communication technology is creating that has vast implications for global society.

References

Davoudi, S., & Fenton, B. (2011, June 24). Guardian chief forecasts years of upheaval. *The Financial Times*, p. 17.

Kruckeberg, D., & Tsetsura, K. (2004). International journalism ethics. In J. C. Merrill & A. De Beer (Eds.), *Global journalism: Topical issues and media systems* (pp. 84–92). New York: Longman.

Valentini, C., & Kruckeberg, D. (2011). Public relations and trust in contemporary global society: A Luhmannian perspective of the role of public relations in enhancing trust among social systems. *Central European Journal of Communication, 4*(1), 89–105.

Index

Printed in the United States
by Baker & Taylor Publisher Services